Creative Ribbon Crafting

Creative Ribbon Crafting

Cheri Saffiote
Grace Taormina
Ann Snuggs
Kelly Henderson

Sterling Publishing Co., New York
A Sterling/Chapelle Book

Chapelle, Ltd.

Owner: Jo Packham
Editor: Ann Bear

Staff: Areta Bingham, Kass Burchett, Rebecca Christensen, Holly Fuller, Marilyn Goff, Amber Hansen, Shirley Heslop, Holly Hollingsworth, Shawn Hsu, Susan Jorgensen, Leslie Liechty, Pauline Locke, Ginger Mikkelsen, Barbara Milburn, Linda Orton, Jamie Pierce, Karmen Quinney, Rhonda Rainey, Leslie Ridenour, Cindy Stoeckl

Photographer: Kevin Dilley for Hazen Photography
Photography Styling: Susan Laws

A special thank you to C.M. Offray & Son, Inc., who provided all ribbons used in this book.

10 9 8 7 6 5 4 3 2 1

First paperback edition published in 2000 by
Sterling Publishing Company, Inc.
387 Park Avenue South, New York, N.Y. 10016
Originally published under the title
Creative Crafting with Ribbons
© 1998 by Chapelle Ltd.
Distributed in Canada by Sterling Publishing
c/o Canadian Manda Group, One Atlantic Avenue, Suite 105
Toronto, Ontario, Canada M6K 3E7
Distributed in Great Britain and Europe by Cassell PLC
Wellington House, 125 Strand, London WC2R 0BB, England
Distributed in Australia by Capricorn Link (Australia) Pty Ltd.
P.O. Box 6651, Baulkham Hills, Business Centre,
NSW 2153, Australia

Printed in China
All rights reserved

Sterling ISBN 0-8069-9705-2 Paper

If you have any questions or comments
please contact:
Chapelle, Ltd., Inc.
P.O. Box 9252
Ogden, UT 84409
(801) 621-2777
(801) 621-2788 Fax

Ribbon Work

The adorned pillows, frames, and elegant keepsakes featured in this book are excellent examples of the beauty that can be achieved when creating by inspiration and mixing together several different techniques and mediums.

Ribbon flowers made with wire edge ribbon create resilient and versatile flowers. Wire-edge ribbon flowers can be shaped and reshaped as desired. The key to ribbon work is maintaining control over the ribbon. Understanding what each ribbon length will do is of utmost importance in creating petals and flowers.

Adding pressed flowers to any project is a fun way to add color. Keep in mind that the colors and the selection of pressed flowers used in this book are simply suggestions. Any number of colors or pressed flowers can be substituted where desired. Please read the general instructions and individual project instructions before starting any project.

Appliqué is a wonderful way to add instant dimension to any craft. Delightful primitive-style patterns combine with various pieces of ribbon, basic embroidery stitches, and antiquing techniques to create quaint images such as little girls celebrating springtime, angels carrying good tidings, and snowmen sporting winter attire.

Explore how easy it is to stamp on ribbons in different widths, colors, and textures to create a variety of craft and home decor projects. With just a few materials and some basic techniques, it is easy to decorate ribbons to create gifts, as well as accessories to compliment the home.

Adhesive ribbon is fun and easy to use. Simply follow manufacturer's instructions to create a quick project. If not available in desired style and color, make your own by applying a thin coat of glue, appropriate for the project, to one side of ribbon. For paper projects, apply rubber cement. Apply a craft glue for wood and craft projects. When working with fabrics, apply a fabric glue to the ribbon.

Let creativity bloom by substituting different ribbons for those suggested and combining flowers to design original arrangements. Experiment and remember, as with all crafts, practice makes perfect. Sometimes the unexpected works out better than the original plan!

Table of

General Instructions 8-15
Cheri Saffiote 16
Cat Cut-Out 17
Angel Gift 20
Rain or Shine 23
Friendship Garden Girl .27
Angel Pillow 31
Merry Heart 33
Peace Angel 35
Snowfolk 38
Snow Cut-Out 40

Grace Taormina 44
Lemon & Chili Bags 45
Kitchen Magnets 48
Green Pillow 49
Bee Stationery 50
Zebra Frame 52
Candlelight 53
Gift Wrap 54
Sweet Home Journal 55
Velvet Pillow 56
Photo Albums 57
Ribbon Topiary 60
Ribbon Quilt 61
Desk Set 62
Oriental Pillows 64
Picture Hanger 65
Very Cherry 66
Fern Journal 68
Checked Hearts Towel 70
Sunflower Journal 71

Contents

Ann Snuggs 72
Bird Bath Picture 73
Initial 77
Potted Salvia 82
Flower Basket 84
Welcome 86
Dogwood Pillow 89
Heart Note Card 92
Flower Handkerchief 94
Tea Cloth 96
Nature's Bookmark 98

Kelly Henderson 99
Stamped Note Card 100
Seeded Eggs 101
Picket Pot 102
Rose Fence 103
Birthday Cake Box 105
Pedestal Dish 107
Pumpkin. 108
Baby Dress 109
Toddler Coat 111
Folding Screen 113
Candle Spray 114
Tapestry Stocking 116
Satin Gazebo 118
Trinket Box 120
Penny Purse 121
Floral Angel 122
Ladybug Gift Bag 125
Apple-a-Day 126
Metric Equivalency Chart 128
Index 128

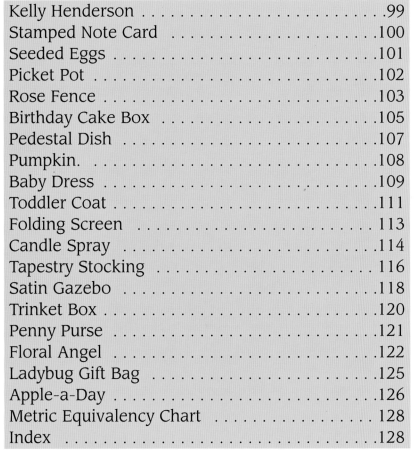

Dimensional Ribbon Work

Folded Leaf

1. Fold ends of one ribbon length forward diagonally.
2. Gather-stitch across bottom edge of folds.
3. Tightly pull gather stitch and secure thread for a completed Folded Leaf.

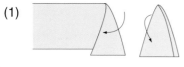

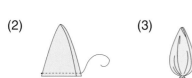

Folded Rose

Thread and knot a small needle with floss to match ribbon and set aside.

1. Using a 8" piece of ribbon, finger-press a 45-degree fold to create an L-shape.
2. Fold and press horizontal leg backward so it extends to the left.
3. Fold vertical leg backward so it extends downward.
4. Fold horizontal leg backward so it extends to the right. Repeat.
5. On reaching ends of ribbon, hold last fold and its leg firmly between thumb and forefinger, letting folded section release itself.

6. Pull other leg gently through folds. Using threaded needle, tack base of rose at center in place for a completed Folded Rose.

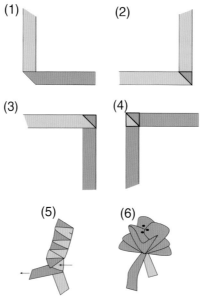

Fork Cut

1. Fold desired ribbon in half lengthwise.
2. Cut end of ribbon diagonally from corner point on selvage edge.
3. Completed Fork Cut.

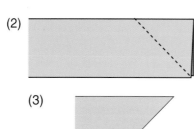

Free Form Flower

1. Use a 2" piece of ribbon. Fold each end under about ⅛". Baste along one long edge of ribbon with one strand of floss.
2. Gently gather ribbon to create a petal as desired.
3. Knot to secure ruffled effect. Stitch ribbon in place along the gathered edge for a completed Free Form Flower.

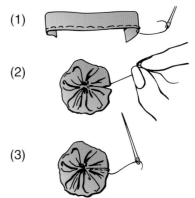

Gather-Stitch

1. Make gather-stitches that are exactly ⅛". If stitches are larger than ⅛", gathers will look like pleats. If stitches are smaller than ⅛", gathers will create large openings when joining petals into a circle.
2. Pull gathering thread as tightly as possible after gather-stitching ribbon. Hold gathers down firmly with one hand while securing thread in place with the other hand.
3. Always adjust gathers so they are evenly spaced.

Knife Pleating

1. Pin ribbon pleats ½" deep and ½" apart, all in the same direction. Press. Secure one long edge of pleated ribbon with adhesive ribbon. Apply to project as indicated for complete Knife Pleating.

Pulled Leaf

1. Fold wired ribbon length in half, matching short ends.
2. Push ½" to ¾" of ribbon back on wires on one edge. Pull wires evenly until completely gathered. Overlap ends of wires. Twist to secure.
3. Open and shape leaf for a completed Pulled Leaf.

(1)

(2)

(3)

Rose

1. Knot one end of length of wired ribbon.
2. At opposite end, gently pull wire from one side to gather. Continue gathering until entire side is completely ruffled and curling naturally. Leave wire end free; do not cut off.
3. To form rose, hold knotted end in one hand and begin to spiral gathered ribbon loosely around knot with other hand. Wrap tightly at first to form a bud, then continue wrapping lightly so that it flares out and acquires an open rose effect. To end, fold raw edge down to meet gathered edge. Secure by wrapping wire length around knot tightly and catching in free end; cut wire end off.
4. Completed Rose.

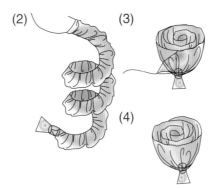

Tendril

1. Holding a length of wired ribbon at one end, begin twisting the ribbon in one direction until tight.
2. Ribbon will twist on itself for a completed Tendril.

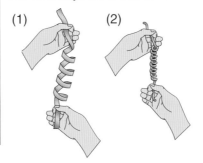

Ending Stitching

Secure stitches in place for each small area. Do not drag ribbon from one area to another. Tie slip knot on wrong side of needlework to secure stitch in place and cut ribbon.

Floss

Floss colors are outlined in project stitch guides. The 6-strand floss should be separated into one or more strands according to project instructions.

Knotting End of Ribbon

1. Pierce end of ribbon with needle, then pierce again.
2. Pull needle and ribbon through holes to form complete knot at end of ribbon.

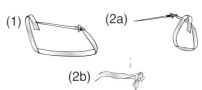

Needles

A size 3 crewel embroidery needle works well for most fabrics when using 4mm ribbon. For 7mm ribbon, use a chenille needle, size 18 to 24. As a rule of thumb, the barrel of the needle must create a hole in fabric large enough for ribbon to pass through. If ribbon does not pull through fabric easily, a larger needle is needed. For hand-sewing, a number 10 sharp needle is recommended on some projects.

Ribbon Tips
Always keep ribbon flat and loose while working stitches. Untwist ribbon often and pull ribbon softly so it lies flat on top of fabric. Be creative with stitching. Exact stitch placement is not critical, but make certain all placement marks are covered.

Threading Ribbon
Thread ribbon through eye of needle. With tip of needle, pierce center of ribbon ¼" from end. Pull needle and ribbon through hole to lock ribbon in place.

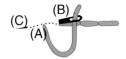

Embroidery Stitches

Backstitch
Come up at A; go down at B, to right of A. Come up at C, to left of A. Repeat B–C, inserting the needle in the same hole for a complete Backstitch.

Blanket Stitch
1.   Bring needle up at A, down at B. Bring needle up again at C, keeping thread under needle.
2.   For second stitch, go down at D and back up at E.

3.   Completed Blanket Stitch.

Cross-Stitch
1.   Come up at A, go down at B.
2.   Come up again at C and down at D, forming an "X" for a completed Cross-Stitch.

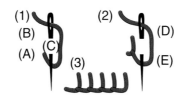

Decorative Lazy Daisy Stitch
1.   Refer to Lazy Daisy Stitch and complete the stitch.
2.   Using ribbon/floss color indicated, come up at E and go down just inside the top of the loop, forming a Straight Stitch inside the Lazy Daisy Stitch.
3.   Completed Decorative Lazy Daisy Stitch.

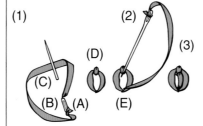

French Knot
1.   Bring needle up at A; smoothly wrap ribbon once around needle unless otherwise indicated.
2.   Hold ribbon securely off to one side, and push needle down at A.
3.   Completed French Knot.

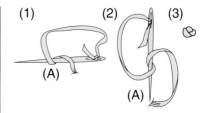

Japanese Ribbon Stitch
1.   Come up through fabric at the starting point of stitch at A. Lay ribbon flat on fabric. At end of stitch, pierce ribbon with needle at B. Slowly, pull length of ribbon through to back, allowing ends of ribbon to curl. If ribbon is pulled too tightly, the effect of the stitch can be lost. Vary petals and leaves by adjusting the length, the tension of ribbon before piercing, and how loosely or tightly ribbon is pulled down through itself.
2.   Completed Japanese Ribbon Stitch.

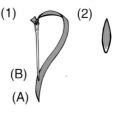

Lazy Daisy Stitch
1.   Bring needle up at A, down at B, and back up at C, leaving a loose loop. Pull needle through. To hold the loop in place, go down on other side at D.
2.   Completed Lazy Daisy Stitch.

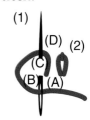

Leaf Stitch

1. For tip of leaf, make small Straight Stitch. Make slanted fly stitches by coming up at A, going down at B, and up again at C.
2. Hold this stitch in place by going down at D. Repeat fly stitches to fill leaf area.
3. Completed Leaf Stitch.

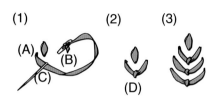

(1) (2) (3)

(A) (B) (C) (D)

Long Stitch

1. Refer to Straight Stitch to complete stitches.
2. Work several stitches that are the same length but alternating placement of every other stitch for completed Long Stitch.

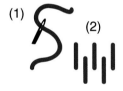

(1) (2)

Outline Stitch

Bring needle up at end of line at A. Keep ribbon/floss to right and above needle. Push needle down at B, and back up at C. Continue until desired length is stitched for a complete Outline Stitch.

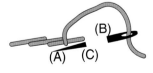

(B) (A) (C)

Padded Satin Stitch

1. Form Satin Stitches slightly shorter than desired finished length.
2. Stitch as many as desired to form padding.
3. Cover padding with second layer of Satin Stitches that are desired length.
4. Completed Padded Satin Stitch.

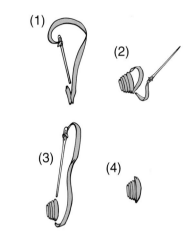

(1) (2) (3) (4)

Padded Straight Stitch

1. Work a Straight Stitch slightly shorter than desired finished length. Then come up at A and go down at B to cover. Keep ribbon flat, loose, and puffy.
2. Completed Padded Straight Stitch.

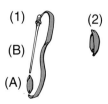

(1) (2) (B) (A)

Running Stitch

Come up at A and go down at B. Repeat for a line of straight stitches with an unstitched area between

each stitch as shown for a complete Running Stitch.

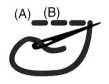

(A) (B)

Satin Stitch

This stitch may be worked vertically, horizontally, or on the diagonal. Stitches may be the same length or graduated.

1. Keep ribbon smooth and flat; come at up at A and go down at B, forming a Straight Stitch. Then come up at C, and down at D forming another Straight Stitch next to the first.
2. Repeat to fill design area for a complete Satin Stitch.

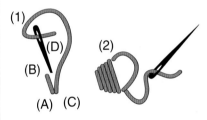

(1) (D) (B) (A) (C) (2)

Spider Web Rose

1. Using two strands of floss, securely work Straight Stitches to form five spokes. These are anchor stitches to create web with ribbon.
2. Bring ribbon up through center of spokes.
3. Weave ribbon over one spoke.
4. Weave under next spoke; continue weaving over then under, in one direction until spokes are covered.

5. Completed Spider Web Rose.

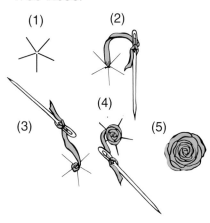

(1) (2) (3) (4) (5)

Stem Stitch

Bring needle up at end of line at A. Keep ribbon to right and below needle. Push needle down at B and back up at C. Continue until desired length is stitched for a complete Stem Stitch.

(A) (C) (B)

Straight Stitch

This stitch may be taut or loose, depending on desired effect.
1. Come up at A. Go down at B; keep ribbon flat.
2. Completed Straight Stitch.

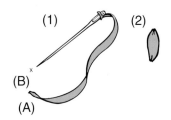

(1) (2) (B) (A)

Fabric Basics

All fabrics used are 100% cotton. Ribbons are described in individual projects' instructions.

Fusible Appliqué

1. Enlarge design to size indicated.
2. Trace reverse of each section of design on non-adhesive (paper) side of double-sided fusible web (outline will be a mirror image of motif). Cut out web motif, allowing a small margin.
3. Using an iron, press unbacked (adhesive) side of web to wrong side of fabric, matching grain lines and following manufacturer's instructions. Cut out motif with sharp fabric scissors.
4. Mark placement of motif on background fabric. Peel paper from web to reveal adhesive. Place motif adhesive side down on marked background fabric. Using an iron, press in place. Repeat Steps 1-4 for all pieces in the design.
5. Finish edges of motif with embroidery stitches.

Pressing Fabric

Many projects require the use of an embroidery hoop for stitching on designs. When embroidery is completed, remove hoop and press lightly around design with a warm iron to remove any indentations.

Tea-dying

Bring to a boil, six to eight tea bags in two quarts of water. Turn off heat and steep for at least 20 minutes. Place fabric in tea and soak for at least 30 minutes. The longer fabric is left in tea, the darker the color. Rinse fabric slightly, wring out, and let dry, outside if possible, as fabric tends to darken and spot more in sunlight.

Pressed Flowers

Pressing Flowers

1. Select only fresh flowers. Cut flowers as soon as they open. Place flower stems in water until ready for pressing. Never press wilted flowers.
2. Be certain flowers are completely dry. If necessary, pat them dry with a paper towel.
3. Cut flowers from stems at base of blossoms.
4. Spread flowers in large old or unwanted book between several pages. Press stems, buds, tendrils, and leaves, as well as blooms of each flower, if possible. Do not overlap any flowers or stems. Flowers need to dry quickly.
5. After placing flowers between pages, close book and weight it down with a heavy object such as a concrete block or large book.
6. Store in a dry place.
7. Flowers will be ready in 7-14 days depending on size and thickness of flowers.

Creativity

1. Look closely at your surroundings for interesting plant material. Grasses, tiny flowers, moss, and other elements work well in designs.

2. Collect short pieces of poetry or prose, thoughts of the day, scripture quotes, or sweet sentiments to add to projects. Look for other creative ways to honor or remember a friend. Add a date to commemorate a special occasion.

Ribbon Amounts

Ribbon amounts called for are based on yardage available on ribbon cards. For example, 2mm comes on 7-yard cards, 4mm on 5-yard cards, and 7mm on 3-yard cards.

Stamping on Ribbon Basics

Embossing

Emboss ribbon using a slow-drying ink (embossing ink or pigment ink) to stamp with, sprinkling the wet image with embossing powder (shaking off excess powder), and then heating the image with an embossing heat tool. Because ink is absorbed into the ribbon, the raised effect may not turn out as it would on paper. Test ribbon before constructing the project.

Wipe a fabric softener dryer sheet along the ribbon before stamping to reduce static cling and eliminate embossing powder sticking to undesired areas of ribbon. Use a small paintbrush to brush away any stray,

Glossary of Flowers

Alyssum

Bachelor Button

Blue Salvia

Blue Hydrangea

Daisy

Fern

Marigold

Larkspur

Lobelia

Phlox

Pink Hydrangea

Queen Anne's Lace

Spirea

Verbena

Viola Johnny-Jump-Up

Yellow Wildflower

clinging powder prior to using the heat tool.

Embossing powders are available in many opaque colors as well as metallic, iridescent, and sparklers, which contain glitter.

Inks

There are a variety of different types of inks and paints available that can be used for stamping. Many are available in the form of an ink pad. A rainbow ink pad offers multiple complementary colors arranged next to each other on one strip. These are useful when a multiple color effect is desired.

If a type of shade of ink is not available in an ink pad, spread ink or paint onto a foam wedge sponge. Apply ink to rubber stamps as with an ink pad.

Most of the projects in this book use textile inks which are specially formulated for use with fabrics. They are permanent and washable.

When using an outline stamp, color in the image with permanent textile markers.

Pigment inks contain an ingredient that makes the ink dry much slower. Colors in pigment-based rainbow pads will not blend with each other, so they stay perfectly separated. These slow-drying inks allow time needed to add embossing powders that need to be heat-set. It is safe to use pigment inks on projects that will not be washed.

Ribbons

Although the end use of the ribbon will determine selection of ribbon color, stamping ink, and paint color, selecting a smooth, light-colored ribbon to stamp on will result in a clearer, more precise impression.

A few projects in this book use textured and/or dark ribbons with some interesting results. When using dark-colored ribbons, make a color test with ink colors before constructing the project, as ribbon color sometimes affects ink color.

Stamps

Rubber stamps come in many shapes and sizes, and are usually mounted on wood, foam, or rollers.

When selecting a stamp, be aware that there are two types to choose from — an outline stamp or a broad surface stamp.

An outline stamp is typically stamped in a dark color and the design is then further embellished and colored in as the crafter desires with various colored markers. A broad surface stamp imprints a solid design that eliminates the need for additional coloring.

Stamps used on projects in this book can easily be replaced with other stamps that are more suitable to the occasion or decor. Many of the photographs feature stamps different from those actually used to offer ideas on how to personalize projects. For example, use a pansy stamp instead of a sunflower for that friend who loves pansies but does not care for those large yellow flowers.

Tool Basics

Fabric Scissors

Designate a pair of scissors for cutting fabrics and non-wire-edge ribbons. Using fabric scissors to cut other materials will dull blades and make them less effective at cutting fabric.

Floss

Floss colors are outlined in project stitch guides. The 6-strand floss should be separated into one or more strands according to project instructions.

Heat Tool

These tools are made specifically for embossing. They get very hot, but do not blow a lot of air, allowing the powder to set to the ink.

Hot Glue Gun & Glue Sticks
Hot glue is best for constructing projects. Use the "cloudy" glue sticks when working with fabric. Clear glue sticks do not penetrate fabric well.

Marking Tools
Marking tools include an air- or water-soluble dressmaker's pen, and an erasable marking pen. They can be found in several colors. Colored pens work well on light-colored fabrics; a white pen is necessary for use on dark or black fabrics.

Use marking tools to mark general placement. Try to use as few marks as possible– too many marks can become confusing.

Soft Rubber Brayer
This brayer is used most commonly for creating back-grounds. Rubber brayers are available in 2", 4", and 6" widths.

Ink the entire surface of the brayer by rolling it over an ink pad or coloring it with brush markers. While the brayer is resting on its handle, apply the markers to the rubber roller as it is turned. Roll the brayer across stamping surface, applying even pressure.

Transferring

Materials
Tracing paper
Transfer paper

Tools
Marking tool:
    disappearing pen;
    dressmaker's pen;
    erasable pen; pencil
Photocopy machine
Scissors: craft; fabric
Straight pins
Tape of choice

1. If directions indicate to enlarge pattern, place pattern directly in photocopy machine. Enlarge required percentage.
2. If using natural light box technique, trace design on a piece of tracing paper or mylar. Tape tracing paper onto a sun-lit window. Hold or tape fabric in place over design and trace design onto fabric with marking tool of choice.

Wood Basics

Painting Techniques
—Base
To base paint an area, apply two to three even coats of acrylic paint. This will ensure best coverage and an even look to paint.

—Dot
Make dots by using a round object such as the end of a paint brush, stylus, corsage pin, etc. Dip in acrylic paint, then touch on project. Create uniform dots by loading painting tool each time a dot is required.

—Splatter-paint
Splatter-painting creates random speckles on project's surface. Use an old toothbrush or similar stiff-bristled brush. Thin acrylic paint with water, load brush, and pull your thumb across bristles, splattering as you go. The thinner the paint, the larger the speckles.

Transferring to Wood
1. Trace enlarged pattern onto a sheet of tracing paper.
2. Place traced pattern onto wood item and secure on one edge with transparent tape.
3. Slip a piece of graphite transfer paper, with graphite side down, between wood and tracing paper. Trace over design using a stylus or inkless ballpoint pen. Use a light touch, as pressing too hard can dent wood or make marks that are hard to cover.
4. Lift off tracing paper and graphite transfer paper.

Cheri Saffiote

In what seemed to be overnight success, Cheri Saffiote revolutionized the craft industry by publishing her primitive tole painting and quilting designs. Her love for designing began many years ago while attending high school where she excelled in all of her arts and crafts classes.

Cheri sold her work at various fairs and in 1988 she decided to make a business out of her hobby by opening a quilt and tole painting store she called Calico Station. One year later, Cheri began to publish her designs. Within three years, she had tripled the size of her store and opened a distribution center for her published work under her trademark Button Button Designs by Cheri. Today, her designs are available through retail stores across the United States and through her own distribution center, Calico Station Distribution.

Cat Cut-Out

Materials

Wood: ⅜"-thick plywood (11" x 20")

Pre-sized ribbon: 1½"-wide yellow/white plaid (scrap); 2½"-wide linen (⅛ yd.)

Wire-edge ribbon: 1½"-wide blue/ivory check (⅜ yd.), green plaid (⅛ yd.), yellow/white plaid (½ yd.); 1⅜"-wide green/ivory check (⅛ yd.)

Acrylic paints: brown/gray, dk. brown, dk. antique gold, dk. gray, ivory

Antiquing paste

Buttons: ¾"-1" red (2)

Cup of coffee

Spray sealer: matte finish

Wire: 30 gauge (⅜ yd.); hanger (¼ yd.)

General Supplies & Tools

Drill and drill bit (⅛")

Fabric marker: disappearing

Gesso

Glue: craft; wood

Needle: hand-sewing

Paintbrushes

Pencil

Permanent marker: #05 tip, black

Paper hole punch: ¼"

Pliers

Sandpaper: fine grit; medium grit

Scissors: craft; fabric

Scroll saw

Thread: coordinating

Toothbrush: old

Soft cloths

Instructions

1. Enlarge Cat Cut-Out Transfer Patterns 1-4 on following page. Using a pencil, trace one cat, one star base, two paws, and two wings on plywood.

2. Using a scroll saw, cut out pattern pieces.

3. Using a drill and drill bit, drill a ⅜" deep hole in top of cat head, between ears.

4. Using fine grit sandpaper, sand all rough edges on wood pieces. Use soft, damp cloth to remove dust.

5. Following manufacturer's instructions, apply Gesso to all wood pieces.

6. Refer to General Instructions for Transferring to Wood on page 15. Enlarge cat face and transfer to wood.

7. Refer to General Instructions for Painting Techniques on page 15 and Cat Cut-Out Placement on page 20. Paint cat, wings, paws, and star base as follows: base — cat body and paws – brown/gray; wings and star base – dk. antique gold; nose – dk. gray.

8. Using medium grit sandpaper, sand all edges and surfaces on painted wood pieces to create a primitive appearance. Use soft, damp cloth to remove dust.

9. Using a soft cloth and following manufacturer's instructions, apply antiquing paste to all painted wood pieces. Wipe off paste with clean, soft cloth.

10. Refer to General Instructions for Painting Techniques. Load an old toothbrush with dk. brown

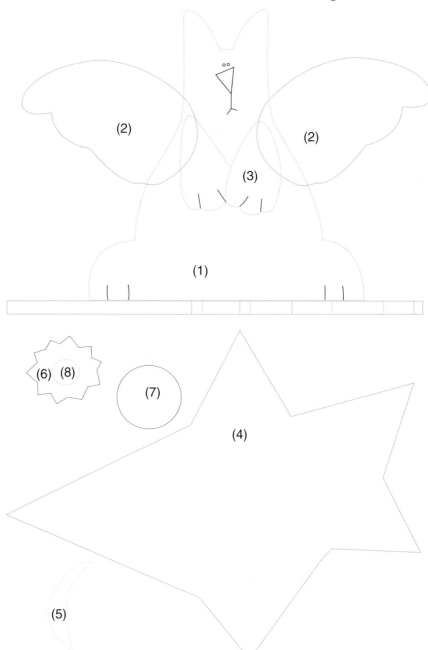

Cat Cut-Out Transfer Patterns   Enlarge 185%

acrylic paint and splatter-paint all pattern pieces. Let paint dry. Clean brush, and repeat process using ivory acrylic paint.

11. Using matte spray

sealer, spray and seal all painted wood pieces.

12. Refer to Cat Cut-Out Transfer Patterns. Enlarge Patterns 5-8. Trace moon, flower, and large circle to linen pre-sized ribbon. Trace small circle to yellow/white plaid pre-sized ribbon. Using fabric scissors, cut out pattern pieces.

13. Dip moon into a cup of coffee to stain. Let dry.

14. Refer to Cat Cut-Out Placement. Using craft glue, attach moon to wing and small circle to center of linen flower. Using black permanent marker, draw stars on wings and stitch lines around moon, flower, small circle, large linen circle, and cat's nose. Draw mouth, paw lines, and eyes on cat.

15. Mark center of hanger wire. Using pliers, shape center of hanger wire into a

Diagram A

1¼"-diameter circle. Twist ends together to form a halo as shown in Cat Cut-Out Placement.

16. Using craft scissors, cut four 3" lengths from 30 gauge wire. Hold wires together as one and twist remaining piece of wire around center of wires to make whiskers as shown in Cat Cut-Out Placement.

17. Using wood glue, attach halo in top of cat's head, whiskers under nose, wings and paws on cat, and cat on star base.

18. Using craft scissors, cut a 12½" length from blue/ivory check wire-edge ribbon. Using a disappearing fabric marker, mark ribbon at 2" intervals, beginning and ending ¼" from raw ends, as shown in Diagram A. Using a

Diagram B

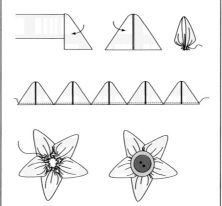

hand-sewing needle and coordinating thread, run a hand-gathering stitch in a semicircular shape within each interval. Tightly pull gathering thread so each petal measures about 1¼". Knot thread to secure. Shape into a flower and tack ends together. Sew a button in center of flower.

19. Using craft scissor, cut five 3½" lengths from yellow/white plaid wire-edge ribbon. Fold each ribbon and sew a gather stitch as shown in Diagram B. Tightly pull thread to form dahlia petals. Knot thread to secure. Tack petals together to form dahlia. Glue large linen circle in center of dahlia. Glue remaining button in center of large linen circle.

20. Stitch green plaid and green/ivory check ribbons into dahlia petals for leaves as shown in Diagram C.

21. Refer to Cat Cut-Out Placement. Glue flowers and leaves to front of cat.

Diagram C

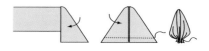

Cat Cut-Out Placement

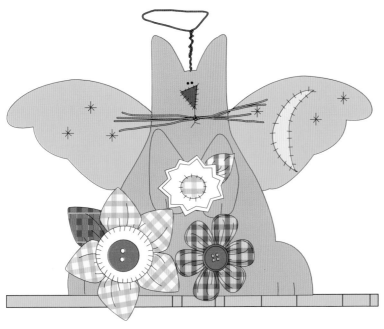

Materials

Fabric: 18" x 13" blue/tan stripe

Embroidery ribbon: 4mm green, orange, pale yellow (1 yd. each)

Grosgrain ribbon: 1½"-wide brown, red (scraps)

Wire-edge ribbon: 1½"-wide peach taffeta (scrap); 2¼"-wide ivory taffeta (½ yd.)

Woven ribbon: 1½"-wide yellow/white plaid (scrap)

Embroidery floss: brown, dk. brown, green, yellow

Double-sided fusible web (⅛ yd.)

General Supplies & Tools

Embroidery hoop
Iron/ironing board
Needle: embroidery
Pencil
Scissors: fabric

Instructions

1. Refer to General Instructions for Tea-dying on page 12. Tea-dye fabric.

2. Refer to General Instructions for Fusible Appliqué on page 12. Enlarge Angel Gift Motifs & Transfer Patterns 1-6 on opposite page. Using a pencil, trace motifs on paper side of fusible web. Using fabric scissors, cut around motifs. Position all ribbons with back sides up on a flat surface. Iron wings to ivory taffeta wire-edge ribbon. Iron face to peach taffeta wire-edge ribbon. Iron star to yellow/white plaid woven ribbon. Iron heart to red grosgrain ribbon. Iron basket to brown grosgrain ribbon. Cut out motifs.

3. Refer to Angel Gift Placement at right. Remove backing from fusible web and fuse motifs to fabric.

4. Refer to General Instructions for Transferring on page 15. Enlarge Angel Gift Motifs & Transfer Pattern and transfer to fabric.

5. Place fabric tightly in embroidery hoop.

6. Refer to General Instructions for Embroidery Stitches on pages 10–12. Using an embroidery needle, embroider fabric following Angel Gift Stitch Guide on following page.

7. Remove fabric from embroidery hoop, press, and frame as desired.

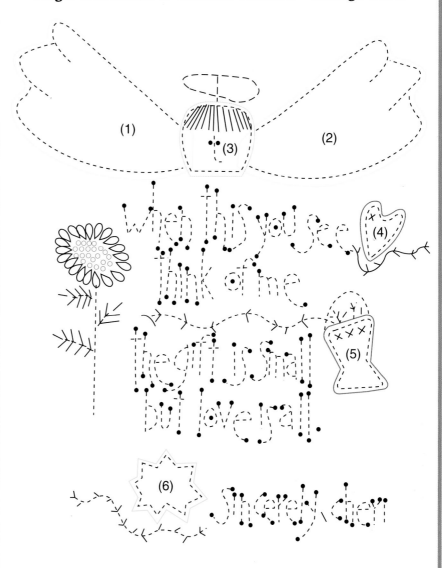

Angel Gift Placement

Angel Gift Stitch Guide

	Description	Ribbon/Floss	Stitch
1.	Wings Outline	dk. brown floss (2 strands)	Running Stitch
2.	Face, Nose Outline	dk. brown floss (2 strands)	Running Stitch
3.	Eyes	dk. brown floss (2 strands)	French Knot
4.	Halo	yellow floss (1 strand)	Running Stitch
5.	Hair	dk. brown & brown floss (3 strands)	Long Stitch
6.	Heart Outline	dk. brown floss (2 strands)	Running Stitch with Cross-Stitch
7.	Basket Outline	dk. brown floss (2 strands)	Running Stitch with Cross-Stitch
8.	Star Outline	dk. brown floss (2 strands)	Running Stitch
9.	Words	dk. brown floss (2 strands)	Running Stitch with French Knot
10.	Vines	green floss (2 strands)	Running Stitch
11.	Vine leaves	green floss (2 strands)	Straight Stitch
12.	Stem	green floss (2 strands)	Running Stitch
13.	Leaves	green ribbon	Leaf Stitch
14.	Flower Petals	orange ribbon	Lazy Daisy Stitch
15.	Flower Center	pale yellow ribbon	French Knot

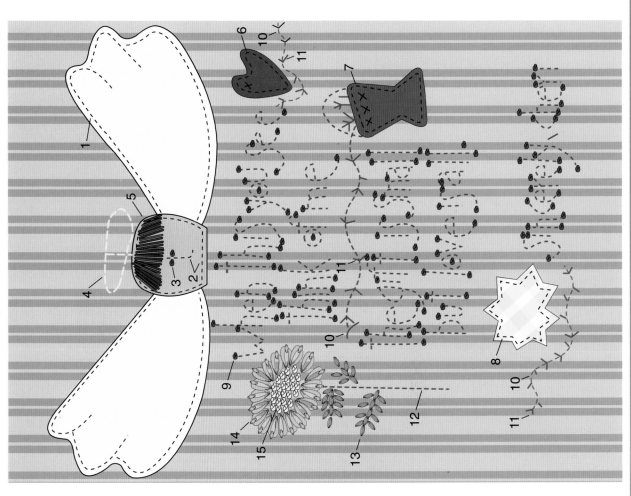

Angel Gift Stitch Guide

General Supplies & Tools

Embroidery hoop
Iron/ironing board
Needle: embroidery; hand-sewing
Paintbrush
Pencil
Permanent marker: #05 tip, black
Scissors: fabric
Sewing machine
Thread: coordinating

Instructions

1. Cut a 13" length and a 1½" x 10" piece from linen ribbon for clouds, ducks, and side border strip. Cut a 1" length from peach woven ribbon for vase flower centers. Set aside. Do not tea-dye.

2. Refer to General Instructions for Tea-dying on page 12. Tea-dye remaining ribbons and fabric.

3. Using fabric scissors, cut royal blue with gold edges, blue/green/red plaid, and blue/green/purple plaid woven ribbons into two equal lengths. Cut two 2" lengths from pale green and burgundy/white check woven

Materials

Fabric: 17" square lt. blue (2)
Linen ribbon: 2"-wide ivory (1 yd.)
Woven ribbon: 1½"-wide antique blue (1 yd.), dk. blue (scrap), royal blue with gold edges (1 yd.), blue/gold plaid (⅜ yd.), blue/green/purple plaid (¼ yd.), blue/green/red plaid (¼ yd.), burgundy/white check (¼ yd.), gold/ white plaid (scrap), pale green (⅜ yd.), mauve (¼ yd.), mauve/white plaid (scrap), peach (¼ yd.)
Embroidery floss: blue, dk. brown, burgundy, gold, gray, green, ivory, mauve, peach, tan, lt. yellow
Acrylic paint: lt. brown
Double-sided fusible web (1 yd.)
Pillow form: 16" square

ribbons. Lay each pair of matching ribbons side-by-side lengthwise, and using a hand-sewing needle and coordinating thread, baste each pair of ribbons together to form proper width for cutting patterns.

4. Cut burgundy/white check woven ribbon to form a 2" square. Cut one 2" length from burgundy/white check woven ribbon, cut one 6½" and one 5¼" length from linen ribbon. Cut one 8" length from pale green woven ribbon, and cut one 8" and two 9⅞" lengths from antique blue woven ribbon for border strips.

5. Refer to General Instructions for Fusible Appliqué on page 12. Enlarge Rain or Shine Motifs & Transfer Patterns 1-33 at right. Using a pencil, trace motifs on paper side of fusible web. Using fabric scissors, cut around motifs. Position all ribbons with back sides up on a flat surface. Iron

clouds and ducks to ivory linen ribbon. Iron sun to gold/white plaid ribbon. Iron outer rainbow layer to blue/green/red plaid ribbon. Iron next rainbow layer to blue/green/purple plaid ribbon. Iron next rainbow layer to pale green ribbon. Iron center of rainbow to

mauve/white plaid ribbon. Iron flowers in vase, small blooming flower, hands, face, and slip to peach ribbon. Iron center of flowers in vase to peach woven ribbon. Iron stockings, duck legs, vase, and center of blooming flowers to tea-dyed linen ribbon. Iron hearts and dress

Rain or Shine Motifs & Transfer Patterns   Enlarge 215%

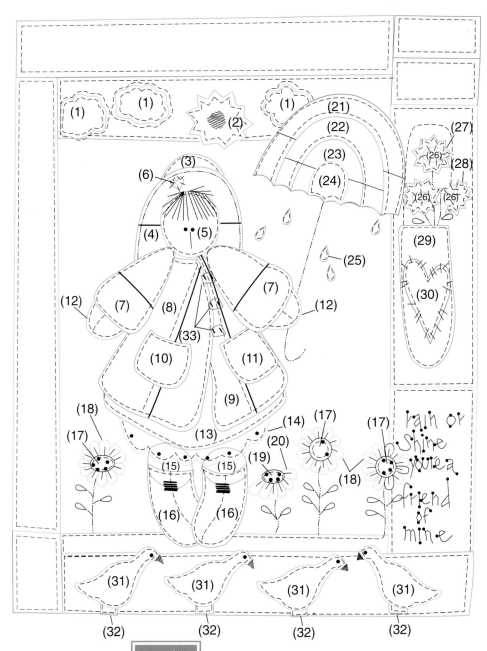

to blue/gold plaid ribbon. Iron boots and hat to antique blue ribbon. Iron hat brim, pockets, sleeves, and raincoat to royal blue with gold edging ribbon. Iron blooming flowers to mauve ribbon. Iron buttons to dk. blue ribbon. Cut out motifs.

6. Apply fusible web to back of ribbon border strips.

7. Refer to Rain or Shine Placement at lower right. Remove backing from fusible web and fuse motifs to one lt. blue fabric square for pillow front in the following order: top antique blue border strips, bottom pale green border strip, linen border strips, burgundy/white check border strips, bottom antique blue border strip, clouds, sun, rainbow (starting at center and working out), vase, large heart, flowers in vase, center of flowers in vase, hat, hands, stockings, boots, slip, dress, raincoat, hat brim, small heart on hat, face, sleeves, pockets, buttons, blooming flowers, center of blooming flowers, duck feet, and ducks.

8. Remove basting stitch from ribbons that were sewn together.

9. Place pillow front tightly in embroidery hoop.

10. Refer to General Instructions for Embroidery Stitches on pages 10–12. Using an embroidery needle, embroider pillow front following photograph and Rain or Shine Stitch Guide on following page.

11. Remove pillow front from embroidery hoop.

12. Using a black permanent marker, write words on border strip. Draw flower near words and stitching on large heart and flowers in vase.

13. With right sides together and ½" seam, machine-sew pillow front to pillow back, leaving a 6" opening at bottom for turning. Clip corners and turn right side out.

14. Insert pillow form. Using a hand-sewing needle and coordinating thread, whip-stitch opening closed.

15. Dilute lt. brown acrylic paint with water. Using a paintbrush, wash diluted paint over design to create an antique appearance.

Rain or Shine Placement

Rain or Shine Stitch Guide

	Description	Floss	Stitch
1.	all motifs	coordinating flosses (2 strands)	Running Stitch
2.	Hair	lt. yellow (2 strands)	Long Stitch
3.	Eyes	dk. brown (2 strands)	French Knot
4.	Nose	dk. brown (2 strands)	Long Stitch
5.	Hat Brim	blue (2 strands)	Outline Stitch
6.	Sun Center	gold (3 strands)	Satin Stitch
7.	Duck Beaks	gold (3 strands)	Satin Stitch
8.	Duck Eyes	dk. brown (2 strands)	French Knot
9.	Stems	green (2 strands)	Stem Stitch
10.	Leaves	green (2 strands)	Lazy Daisy Stitch
11.	Boot Buttons	dk. brown (3 strands)	Satin Stitch
12.	Umbrella Handle	dk. brown (2 strands)	Outline Stitch
13.	Blooming Flower Centers	dk. brown and tan (2 strands)	French Knot
14.	Blooming Flower Petals	mauve (2 strands)	Long Stitch
15.	Hearts Outline	dk. brown (2 strands)	Straight Stitch
16.	Vase Flower Centers	dk. brown (2 strands)	Straight Stitch
17.	Slip	peach (2 strands)	French Knot

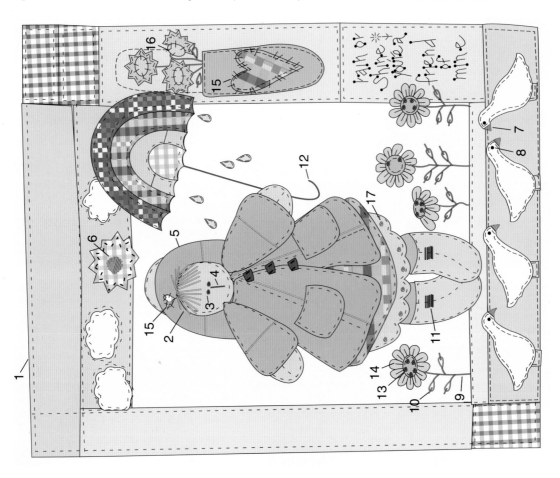

Materials

Fabric: 26" square ivory;
   black (scrap); muslin
   (¼ yd.)
Embroidery ribbon: 2mm
   olive green (1 yd.); 4mm
   lt. blue, pale green, ivory,
   peach, pale pink, lt. purple
   (1 yd. each); 7mm lt. moss
   green, gold (1 yd. each)
Grosgrain ribbon: 1½"-wide
   brown (¼ yd.), mauve
   (scrap), dk. rose (⅛ yd.)

Linen ribbon: 2½"-wide ivory
   (1 yd.)
Satin ribbon: 1½"-wide ivory
   (⅛ yd.)
Embroidery floss: black,
   brown, green, ivory,
   lt. peach
Double-sided fusible web
   (½ yd.)

General Supplies & Tools

Iron/ironing board
Needles: chenille; embroidery
Pencil
Permanent marker: #05 tip,
   black
Scissors: fabric

Instructions

1. Using fabric scissors, cut a 12" length from linen ribbon. Cut a 3" square from muslin fabric. Refer to General Instructions for Tea-dying on page 12. Tea-dye ribbon and fabric.

2. Cut a 2½" length from lt. blue, lt. moss green, pale green, peach, and pale pink embroidery ribbons. Cut another 3" square of muslin fabric. Apply double-sided fusible web to muslin fabric following manufacturer's instructions. Lay ribbons side-by-side in the following order: lt. blue, peach, pale green, lt. moss green, pale pink. Remove backing from fusible web and fuse muslin fabric to ribbons. Cut fused ribbon piece into two 1" x 1¼" rectangles for stockings.

3. Cut a 1½" length from lt. moss green, olive green, ivory, pale pink, and gold embroidery ribbons. Cut two

Friendship Garden Girl Motifs & Transfer Patterns
Enlarge 200%

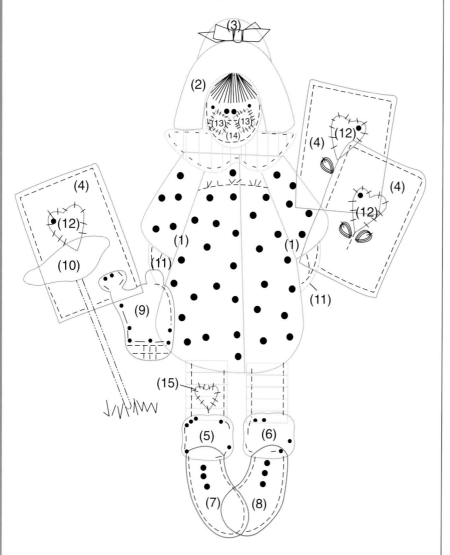

(3)

(2)

(13) (13)
(14)

(4) (12)

(4)

(12)

(4)

(12)

(1) (1)

(10)

(11) (11)

(9)

(15)

(5) (6)

(7) (8)

side of fusible web. Cut around motifs. Position all ribbons with back sides up on a flat surface. Iron dress pieces, hat brim, and hat to linen ribbon. Iron boot cuffs and three seed packets to tea-dyed linen ribbon. Iron boots to brown grosgrain ribbon. Iron watering can and two cheeks to tea-dyed muslin fabric. Iron bird to black fabric. Iron hands and face to satin ribbon. Iron two large hearts to dk. rose grosgrain ribbon. Iron one large heart and one small heart to mauve grosgrain ribbon. Iron collar to fused ribbon piece. Cut out all motifs.

5. Refer to Friendship Garden Girl Placement on page 29. Remove backing from fusible web and fuse motifs to ivory fabric in the following order: kindness seed packet, dk. rose heart, friendship seed packet, mauve heart, heartwarming seed packet, dk. rose heart, bird, stockings, small mauve heart, boots, boot cuffs, hands, dress pieces, watering can, collar, face, hat, and hat brim.

6. Using a black permanent marker, outline hat, hat brim, dress, cuffs, watering can,

1½" lengths from lt. blue, pale green, peach, and lt. purple. Cut a 2" square of muslin fabric. Apply double-sided fusible web to muslin fabric following manu-facturer's instructions. Lay ribbons side-by-side in the following order: lt. purple, lt. blue, peach, pale green, lt. moss green, pale pink, ivory, olive green, gold, lt. purple,

lt. blue, peach, and pale green. Remove backing from fusible web and fuse muslin fabric to ribbons.

4. Refer to General Instructions for Fusible Appliqué on page 12. Enlarge Friendship Garden Girl Motifs & Transfer Patterns 1-15 above. Using a pencil, trace motifs on paper and write words on seed packets following Friendship Garden Girl Placement.

7. Place fabric tightly in embroidery hoop. Refer to General Instructions for Embroidery Stitches on pages 10–12. Using chenille and embroidery needles, embroider design following Friendship Garden Girl Stitch Guide below and on following page. Tie a small bow using peach ribbon. Tack bow on hat using olive green ribbon.

8. Remove from embroidery hoop. Frame as desired.

Friendship Garden Girl Placement

Friendship Garden Girl Stitch Guide

Description	Ribbon/Floss	Stitch
1. Heart Outline	black floss (2 strands)	Straight Stitch
2. Lg. Heart Button	ivory floss (3 strands)	French Knot
3. Heart Stem	green floss (2 strands)	Running Stitch
4. Heart Leaves	green floss (3 strands)	Decorative Lazy Daisy Stitch
5. Seed Packet Outline	black floss (2 strands)	Running Stitch
6. Bird Stick	black floss (6 strands)	Stem Stitch
7. Grass	green floss (3 strands)	Straight Stitch
8. Watering Can Outline	brown floss (2 strands)	Running Stitch with French Knot
9. Watering Can Base	brown floss (2 strands)	Backstitch
10. Boot Cuffs	brown floss (2 strands)	Running Stitch with French Knot
11. Boot Outline	black floss (2 strands)	Running Stitch
12. Boot Button	black floss (6 strands)	French Knot
13. Stocking Outline	olive green ribbon	Running Stitch
14. Dress Polka Dots	all ribbons	French Knot
15. Dress Bodice	olive green ribbon	Straight Stitch
16. Collar Outline	olive green ribbon	Running Stitch
17. Face & Hand Outline	lt. peach floss (2 strands)	Running Stitch

Friendship Garden Girl Stitch Guide (cont.)

Description	Ribbon/Floss	Stitch
18. Cheek Outline	lt. peach floss (2 strands)	Straight Stitch with French Knot in corner
19. Bangs	brown floss (3 strands)	Long Stitch
20. Eyes	black floss (3 strands)	French Knot

Friendship Garden Girl Stitch Guide

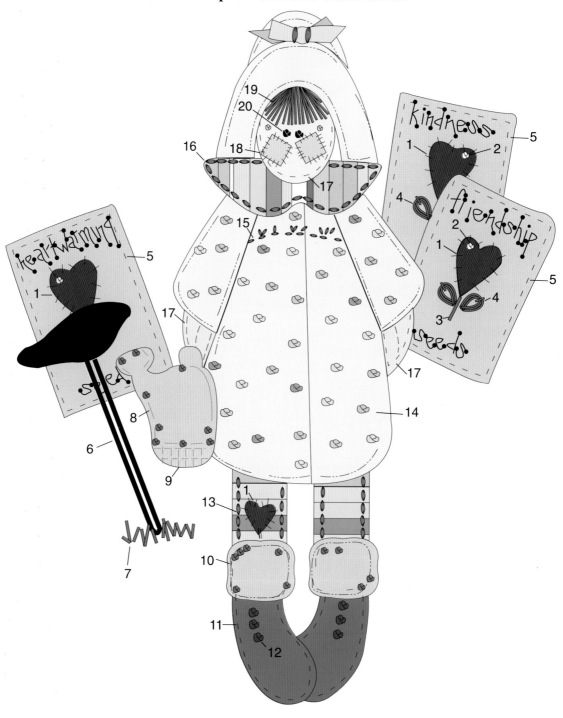

Materials
Fabric: 8½" x 13½" white (2);
  8" x 5" green/tan plaid
Embroidery ribbon: 4mm
  green (1½ yds.), dk. red
  (3 yds.)
Woven ribbon: 2½"-wide ivory
  (½ yd.)
Buttons: ¾" brown (4)
Embroidery floss: brown,
  green, ivory, gold
Double-sided fusible web
  (½ yd.)
Stuffing

General Supplies & Tools
Embroidery hoop
Iron/ironing board
Needles: chenille;
  embroidery; hand-sewing
Pencil
Scissors: fabric
Sewing machine
Thread: coordinating

Instructions
1. Refer to General
Instructions for Tea-dying on
page 12. Tea-dye white fabric
for pillow front and back.

2. Refer to General
Instructions for Fusible
Appliqué on page 12.
Enlarge Angel Motifs &
Transfer Patterns 1-8 on
following page. Using a
pencil, trace motifs to paper
side of fusible web. Using
fabric scissors, cut around
motifs. Position woven
ribbon and fabric with back
sides up on a flat surface.
Iron feet, hand, head, and
wings to ivory woven ribbon.
Iron arm and body to green
plaid fabric. Cut out motifs.

3. Refer to Angel Pillow
Placement on following
page. Remove backing from
fusible web. Fuse motifs to
pillow front.

4. Refer to General
Instructions for Transferring
to Fabric on page 15. Using
enlarged Angel Pillow
Motifs & Transfer Patterns,
transfer wreath and halo to
pillow front.

5. Place pillow front tightly
in embroidery hoop.

6. Refer to General Instructions for Embroidery Stitches on pages 10–12. Using chenille and embroidery needles, embroider pillow front following Angel Pillow Stitch Guide at right.

7. Remove pillow front from embroidery hoop.

8. With right sides together and a ¼″ seam, machine-sew pillow front and pillow back together, leaving a 4″ opening along bottom seam. Clip corners and turn right side out.

9. Stuff pillow to desired firmness. Using a hand-sewing needle and coordinating thread, whip-stitch opening closed.

10. Using three strands of brown embroidery floss, sew a button in each corner of pillow front. Tie ends of floss

Angel Pillow Placement

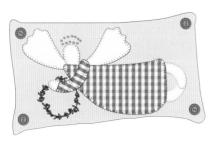

Angel Pillow Motifs & Transfer Patterns   Enlarge 245%

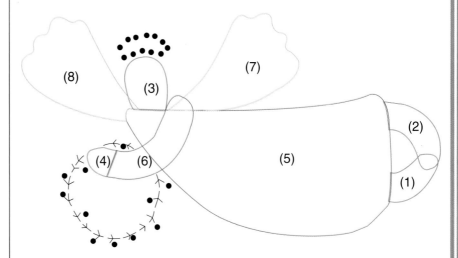

Angel Pillow Stitch Guide

	Description	Ribbon/Floss	Stitch
1.	Halo	gold floss (6 strands)	French Knot
2.	Holly Leaves	green ribbon	Straight Stitch
3.	Berries	dk. red ribbon	French Knot
4.	Wing Outline	gold floss (2 strands)	Blanket Stitch
5.	Head, Hand, Feet Outline	ivory floss (2 strands)	Blanket Stitch
6.	Body, Arm Outline	green floss (2 strands)	Blanket Stitch

Angel Pillow Stitch Guide

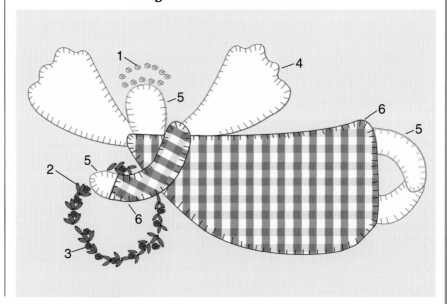

Merry Heart

Materials

Fabric: ivory/tan, 8½" x 13½"
(2); burgundy/tan plaid
9" square (1)
Embroidery ribbon: 4mm
burgundy (2 yds.)
Woven ribbon: 1½"-wide
ivory/red check (¼ yd.);
2"-wide ivory with gold
edges (¼ yd.)
Buttons: ¾" burgundy (4)
Embroidery floss: burgundy,
green, ivory, gold

Double-sided fusible web
(½ yd.)
Stuffing

General Supplies & Tools

Embroidery hoop
Iron/ironing board
Needles: chenille;
embroidery; hand-sewing
Pencil
Scissors: fabric
Sewing machine
Thread: coordinating

Instructions

1. Refer to General
Instructions for Tea-dying on
page 12. Tea-dye ivory/tan
fabric for pillow front and
pillow back, burgundy/tan
plaid fabric, and ivory/red
check woven ribbon.

2. Using fabric scissors, cut
ivory with gold edges woven
ribbon into two equal
lengths. Refer to General
Instructions for Running
Stitch on page 11. Place
ribbons wrong sides together
and gold edges matching.
Using an embroidery needle
and two strands of ivory
floss, hand-sew ribbons
together with a running
stitch. Do not open seam;
press seam flat against one
side of ribbon.

3. Cut ivory/red check
ribbon into two equal
lengths. Lay ribbons
side-by-side, slightly
overlapping edges. Using a
hand-sewing needle and
coordinating thread, tack
ribbons together.

4. Refer to General
Instructions for Fusible

Appliqué on page 12. Enlarge Merry Heart Motifs & Transfer Patterns 1-3 below. Using a pencil, trace motifs on paper side of fusible web. Cut around motifs. To back sides of ribbons and fabric, iron star to ivory with gold edges woven ribbon, small heart to ivory/red check woven ribbon, and large heart to burgundy/tan plaid fabric. Cut out motifs.

5. Refer to Merry Heart Placement at right. Remove backing from fusible web and fuse motifs to pillow front.

6. Refer to General Instructions for Transferring to Fabric on page 15. Using enlarged Merry Heart Motifs & Transfer Patterns below, transfer words, vine, and small heart "buttons" to pillow front.

7. Place pillow front tightly in embroidery hoop.

8. Refer to General Instructions for Embroidery Stitches on pages 10–12. Using chenille and embroidery needles, embroider pillow front following Merry Heart Stitch Guide on opposite page.

9. Remove pillow front from embroidery hoop.

10. With right sides together and a ¼" seam, machine-sew pillow front and pillow back together, leaving a 4" opening along bottom seam. Clip corners. Turn right side out.

11. Stuff pillow to desired firmness. Using a hand-sewing needle and coordinating thread, whip-stitch opening closed.

12. Using three strands of burgundy embroidery floss, sew a button in each corner of pillow front. Tie ends of floss into a knot on top of button.

Merry Heart Motifs & Transfer Patterns   Enlarge 180%

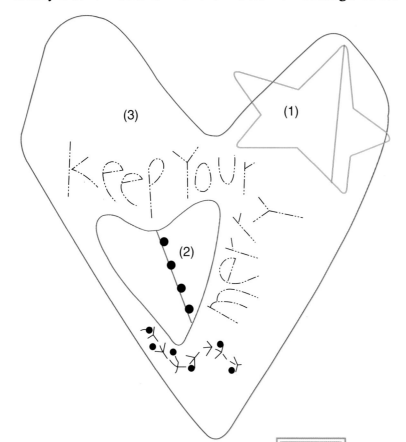

Merry Heart Placement

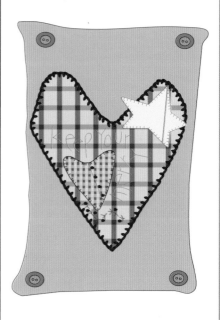

Merry Heart Stitch Guide

	Description	Ribbon/Floss	Stitch
1.	Words	gold floss (3 strands)	Stem Stitch
2.	Vine Leaves	green floss (2 strands)	Straight Stitch
3.	Berries	burgundy floss (3 strands)	French Knot
4.	Small Heart Outline	burgundy floss (2 strands)	Blanket Stitch
5.	Small Heart Button	burgundy ribbon	French Knot
6.	Star Outline	ivory floss (2 strands)	Blanket Stitch
7.	Lg. Heart Outline	burgundy ribbon	Blanket Stitch

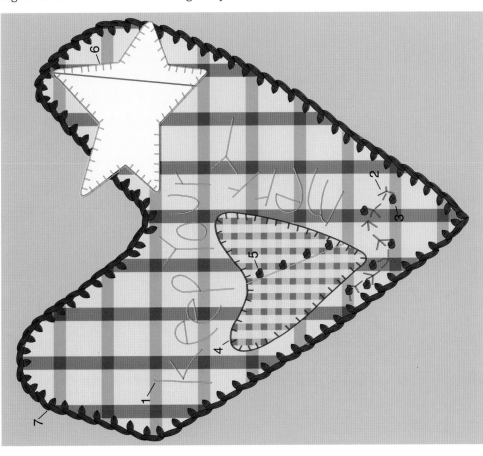

Peace Angel

Materials

Fabric: muslin (¼ yd.)
Linen ribbon: 2¼"-wide ivory (⅛ yd.)
Woven ribbon: ½"-wide

yellow/white plaid (scrap), burgundy (scrap); ¾"-wide Christmas plaid (⅝ yd.); 1¼"-wide burgundy/ivory plaid (⅛ yd.); 1½"-wide burgundy/green plaid with gold edges (⅓ yd.)
Embroidery floss: burgundy, green

Acrylic paints: black, burgundy, golden brown, ivory
Double-sided fusible web
Stuffing
Thread: metallic gold
Twigs: 13"-15" grapevine (14)
Wire: hanger (⅓ yd.)

General Supplies & Tools

Glue gun and glue sticks
Needles: embroidery; hand-
  sewing
Paintbrush
Pencil
Permanent marker: #05 tip,
  black
Pliers
Scissors: fabric
Sewing machine
Thread: coordinating

Instructions

1. Using fabric scissors, cut ivory linen ribbon into a 2¼" square. Refer to General Instructions for Tea-Dying on page 12. Tea-dye ribbon.

2. Cut burgundy/ivory plaid woven ribbon into two equal lengths. Lay ribbons side-by-side, slightly overlapping one long edge. Using a hand-sewing needle and coordinating thread, sew ribbons together to form a 2½" square.

3. Enlarge Peace Angel Motifs & Transfer Patterns on opposite page. Using a pencil, trace two angels on muslin fabric for angel front and angel back. Cut out angels.

4. Using a black permanent marker, draw stars, vine, and nose on angel front, and stars and words on linen ribbon square following Peace Angel Placement on page 38.

5. Refer to General Instructions for Fusible Appliqué on page 12. Using enlarged Peace Angel Motifs & Transfer Patterns 1-3 on opposite page, trace heart, star, and leaves on paper side of fusible web. Cut around motifs. Position all ribbons with back sides up on a flat surface. Iron star to yellow/white plaid ribbon, heart to burgundy ribbon, and leaves to Christmas plaid ribbon. Cut out motifs.

6. Refer to Peace Angel Placement. Remove paper backing from fusible web and fuse motifs to angel front.

7. Refer to General Instructions for Outline Stitch on page 11. Outline-stitch around star using metallic gold thread.

8. Refer to General

Peace Angel Motifs & Transfer Patterns   Enlarge 150%

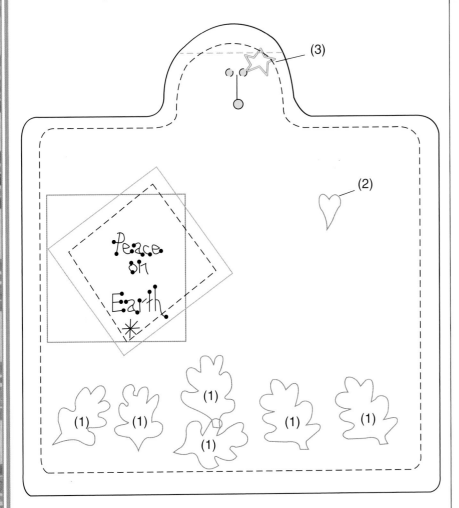

11. Using pliers, shape center of hanger wire into a 1"-diameter circle. Twist ends together to form a halo.

12. Using a glue gun and glue sticks, shape one grapevine twig into a 2"-diameter circle and glue to secure.

13. Hold 12 grapevine twigs together as one. Center twigs over circle twig. Wrap remaining grapevine twig around twigs and weave through circle to form wings as shown in Diagram A.

Diagram A

Using an embroidery needle and six strands of burgundy floss, tack wings 1" below neck on back of angel.

14. Tie a 7" length of burgundy floss into a loop around base of halo for hanger. Hot-glue halo to back of angel head.

15. Tie burgundy/green plaid with gold edged ribbon into a bow around neck of angel.

Instructions for Running Stitch on page 11. Using an embroidery needle, six strands of green floss, and a running stitch, sew burgundy/ivory ribbon square to angel front. Diagonally place and sew linen ribbon square over burgundy/ivory square using six strands of burgundy floss.

9. With right sides together, sew angel front and angel back together, leaving a 2½" opening at bottom for turning. Turn right side out. Stuff to desired firmness. Using a hand-sewing needle and coordinating thread, whip-stitch opening closed.

10. Refer to General Instructions for Painting Techniques on page 15 and Peace Angel Placement. Paint angel front as follows: base — hair golden brown; mouth burgundy; dot — eyes black; berries on vine black and burgundy; eyes ivory.

Peace Angel Placement

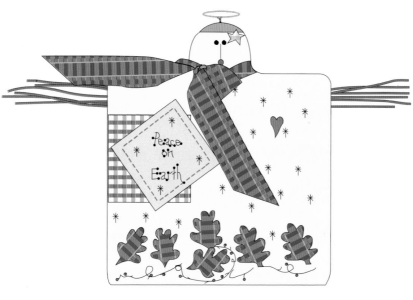

Materials

Fabric: coordinating
(16½" x 9" for small);
coordinating (11½" x 20¼"
for large)

Ribbons: ⅞"- 2⅝"-wide variety
of 8-10 coordinating
grosgrain, linen, and
woven (⅛ yd. - 1½ yds. each
for each pillow)

Buttons: ¼"-⅜" mismatched
(3 for each pillow)

Embroidery floss: black,
blue, gold, ivory

Stuffing

Quilt batting: lightweight
(¼ yd. for small), (⅜ yd. for
large)

General Supplies & Tools

Needles: embroidery; hand-
sewing

Pins

Sewing machine

Scissors: fabric

Thread: coordinating

Small Pillow Instructions

1. Refer to General
Instructions for Tea-dying on
page 12. Tea-dye all fabrics
and ribbons.

2. Using scissors, cut
ribbons into lengths as in
Snowfolk (Small Pillow)
Pattern on page 40, adding
½" to all ribbon ends for
seams.

3. Lay ribbons as shown to form snowman and border, overlapping as necessary to form a 16½" x 9" pillow front. Top-stitch ribbons together.

4. Refer to General Instructions for Satin Stitch on page 11. Using an embroidery needle and two strands of gold embroidery floss, satin-stitch snowman's nose in shape of a carrot as shown in Snowfolk Placement. Using two strands of black embroidery floss, sew buttons on snowman. Refer to General Instructions for French Knot on page 10. Using two strands of black embroidery floss, stitch eyes and mouth with French knots.

5. Cut quilt batting same size as pillow front. Lay pillow front on top of quilt batting and pin together.

6. Refer to General Instructions for Running Stitch on page 11. Using one strand of ivory embroidery floss, sew a running stitch down middle of outside ribbon borders.

7. With right sides together and a ¼" seam, sew pillow front and coordinating fabric together, leaving a 4" opening along bottom seam. Clip corners. Turn right side out.

8. Stuff pillow to desired firmness. Using a hand-sewing needle and coordinating thread, whip-stitch opening closed.

Large Pillow Instructions
1. Repeat Steps 1 and 2 above, referring to Snowfolk (Large Pillow) Pattern for ribbon measurements.

2. With right sides together, sew ribbons 1 and 3 to 2 forming block A; sew ribbons 5 and 7 to 6 forming block C; sew ribbon 8 to 9 forming block D; sew ribbons 10 and 12 to 11 forming block E.

3. With right sides together, sew block A to B; sew block C to B; sew block C to D; sew block D to E; sew block E to F; and, sew block F to G.

4. With right sides together, sew right, left, top, and bottom border strips around snowman to form an 11½" x 20¼" pillow front.

5. Repeat Small Pillow Instructions Steps 4-8, using blue embroidery floss for running stitch.

Snowfolk (Small Pillow) Placement

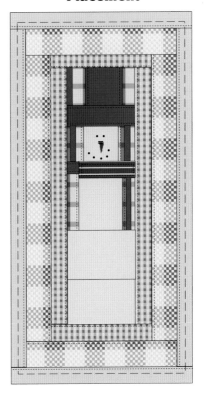

Snowfolk (Large Pillow) Placement

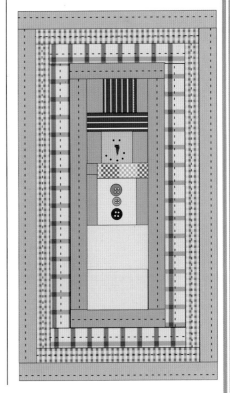

Snowfolk (Small Pillow) Pattern

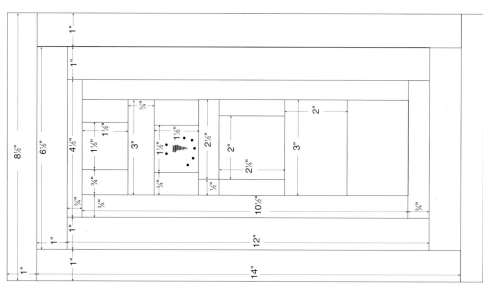

Snowfolk (Large Pillow) Pattern

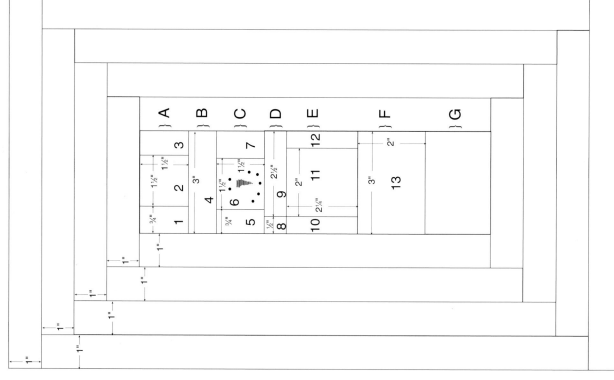

Snow Cut-Out

Materials

Wood: ⅜"-thick plywood (14" x 25")

Pre-sized ribbon: 1⅜"-wide green/tan check (⅛ yd.), green/red/tan check (¼ yd.)

Wire-edge ribbon: ⅞"-wide burgundy/ ivory check (⅜ yd.); 1½"-wide green plaid (⅛ yd.), yellow/white plaid (⅛ yd.)

Acrylic paints: dk. brown, burgundy, gold, green, ivory, red, tan, yellow

Antiquing paste

Dowel: ⅛"-diameter (7½")

Embroidery floss: ivory

Spray sealer: matte finish

Twigs: 4"-5" (2)

General Supplies & Tools

Craft knife
Drill and drill bit (⅛")
Gesso
Glue: craft; wood
Needles: embroidery; hand-
  sewing
Paintbrushes
Pencil
Permanent marker: #05 tip,
  black
Paper hole punch: ¼"
Sandpaper: fine grit; medium
  grit
Scissors: fabric
Scroll saw
Thread: coordinating
Toothbrushes: old (2)
Soft cloths

Instructions

1. Enlarge Snow Cut-Out Patterns on following page. Using patterns 1-3 and a pencil, trace one snowman, two birds, and three pine trees on plywood.

2. Using a scroll saw, cut out pattern pieces. Cut remaining plywood into a 13" x 4" piece for project base.

3. Using a drill and drill bit, drill a ⅜" deep hole in bottom of snowman, at arm level on each side of snowman, and in bottom of

each pine tree. Drill four holes into base, referring to Snow Cut-Out Placement on page 43.

4. Using a craft knife, cut dowel into the following lengths: ⅝", 1⅞", 1⅝", and 3⅜".

5. Using fine grit sandpaper, sand all rough edges on wood pieces, dowel lengths, and base. Remove dust with soft, damp cloth.

6. Following manufacturer's instructions, apply gesso to all wood surfaces.

7. Refer to General Instructions for Transferring to Wood on page 15. Transfer snowman face and coat to wood.

8. Refer to General Instructions for Painting Techniques on page 15 and Snow Cut-Out Placement. Paint snowman, trees, and birds as follows: base, snowman face, lower body, and project base ivory; coat burgundy; fur trim on coat and hat tan; carrot nose gold; pine trees green; birds red; beaks yellow.

9. Using medium grit sandpaper, sand all edges and surfaces on painted wood pieces and dowels to create a primitive appearance. Remove dust with soft, damp cloth.

10. Using a soft cloth and following manufacturer's instructions, apply antiquing paste to all painted wood pieces and dowels. Wipe off paste with clean, soft cloth.

11. Refer to General Instructions for Painting

Techniques. Load an old toothbrush with dk. brown acrylic paint and splatter-paint all painted wood pieces. Let paint dry. Clean brush, and repeat process using ivory acrylic paint.

12. Using matte spray sealer, spray and seal all painted wood pieces.

13. Refer to Snow Cut-Out Patterns at lower left. Using

enlarged patterns 4-7, trace one star (5) and pocket (4) to green/red/tan check pre-sized ribbon. Trace three stars (6) to green/tan check pre-sized ribbon. Trace five stars (7) to yellow/white plaid wire-edge ribbon. Using fabric scissors, cut out stars.

14. Using paper hole punch, punch 19 holes in green/red/tan check pre-sized ribbon to make ornaments on one pine tree.

15. Using craft glue and referring to Snow Cut-Out Placement, attach stars and ornaments to pine trees and pocket to snowman. Using permanent black marker, draw stitches around stars, ornaments, pocket, coat and hat trim. Outline nose and dot eyes with marker.

16. Cut green plaid wire-edge ribbon into one 4½" length. Remove wire from one edge of ribbon. Using a hand-sewing needle and coordinating thread, fold ribbon in half and sew a ¼" seam as shown in Diagram A on opposite page. Sew a gather stitch around top edge of ribbon where wire was removed. Tightly gather ribbon to form a cap and secure thread.

Snow Cut-Out Patterns   Enlarge 190%

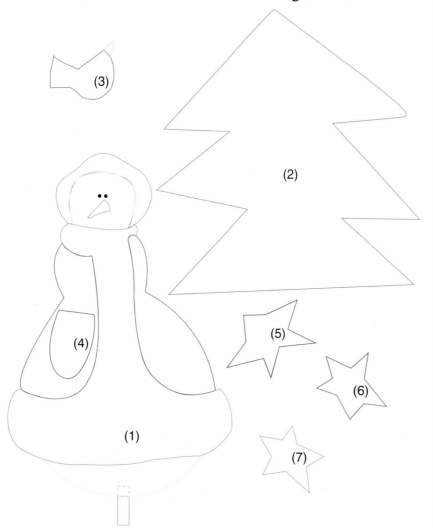

17. Cut a 5" length from ivory embroidery floss. Fold floss in half and tie a knot at folded end as shown in Diagram B. Tack knot of floss to top of cap as shown in Snow Cut-Out Placement. Glue cap to snowman's head.

18. Cut burgundy/ivory check wire-edge ribbon into one 10½" length. Turn ribbon ends up ¼" and fold over ¼" again to hem.

19. Cut six 4" lengths from ivory embroidery floss. Tie knot 1½" from one end, and thread knotted floss in embroidery needle. Insert needle up through hem of one ribbon end. Make a small stitch at top of hem and bring needle back down. Remove needle from floss and knot floss end at base of ribbon for scarf tassels as shown in Diagram C. Repeat process with remaining floss lengths, sewing three lengths to each end of ribbon as shown in Diagram D.

20. Using a clean, dry toothbrush, brush ends of floss to separate floss strands. Tie ribbon scarf around neck of snowman.

21. Referring to Snow Cut-Out Placement and using wood glue, attach birds to pine trees. Glue dowels in holes in base, pine trees and snowman on dowels, and twig branches in snowman for arms.

Diagram A

Diagram B

Diagram C   **Diagram D**

Snow Cut-Out Placement

Grace Taormina

Grace Taormina, Director of Creative Research & Development for Rubber Stampede, is responsible for developing and testing new products and creating projects with rubber stamps. Rubber Stampede, is a California-based manufacturer and worldwide distributor of rubber stamps and stamping accessories.

Grace promotes the art and craft of stamping by conducting workshops and demonstrations at major trade shows and conventions throughout the United States as well as in Japan. Her work has been published in several how-to books and pamphlets as well as numerous trade and consumer publications such as *Better Homes & Gardens*.

Lemon & Chili Bags

Lemon Bag Materials

Fabric: burlap (⅜ yd.)
Linen ribbon: 2½"-wide (½ yd.)
Markers, textile: green, yellow
Paper: 5½" square brown
   butcher; 2¾" square brown
   corrugated (2)
Grommets: gold (2)
Stamp: lemon
String (1 yd.)
Textile ink: black
Twine (1 yd.)

General Supplies & Tools

Glue: craft
Grommet tool
Iron/ironing board
Needles: large-eyed
Pen
Scissors: fabric
Sewing machine
Thread: coordinating

Instructions

1. Cut two 16" x 10" rectangles from burlap.

2. Cut a 16" length from linen ribbon.

3. Using black textile ink, stamp lemons along length of ribbon. Allow ink to dry.

4. Using textile markers, color lemons yellow and leaves green.

5. Center and pin ribbon to top of one piece of burlap. Using a sewing machine, top-stitch along edges of ribbon.

6. Using a grommet tool and following manufacturer's instructions, center and attach grommets ½" apart and 4" from top edge of ribbon.

7. Place right sides of burlap together. With a ½" seam allowance, machine stitch along sides and bottom. Clip corners and, using iron, press seams open.

8. Fold top edge of bag under ¼" and press. Fold and press again. Stitch close to folded hem edge and turn right side out.

9. Thread twine in large-eyed needle and slip down through one grommet and burlap, around and up through opposite side of burlap and grommet. Pull twine to gather bag and tie into a bow.

10. Fold butcher paper in half to form a triangle as shown in Lemon & Chili Bags Card Diagram below. Unfold and fold in half to form a rectangle. Unfold and fold in half on opposite side to form another rectangle. Unfold and push in sides so paper folds down into a square gift tag.

11. Write desired message or recipe on tag.

12. Cut string in half. Glue a string to front and back of tag as shown in Lemon & Chili Bags Card Diagram. Glue corrugated squares on front and back of folded tag, covering string. Tie tag securely to bag.

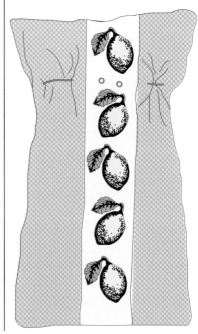

Lemon Bag Placement

Lemon & Chili Bags Card Diagram

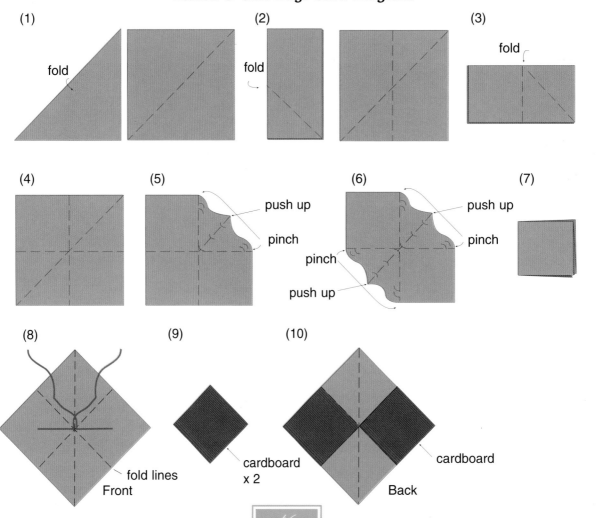

(1) fold

(2) fold

(3) fold

(4)

(5) push up — pinch

(6) push up — pinch — pinch — push up

(7)

(8) fold lines — Front

(9) cardboard x 2

(10) cardboard — Back

46

Chili Bag Materials

Fabric: burlap (¼ yd.)

Linen ribbon: 2½"-wide
(¼ yd.)

Paper: 4" square brown
butcher; 2" square brown
corrugated (2)

Grommets: red (2)

Stamp: chili peppers

String (½ yd.)

Textile ink: black

Twine (1 yd.)

General Supplies & Tools

Glue: craft

Grommet tool

Iron/ironing board

Needles: large-eyed

Markers, textile: green, red

Scissors: fabric

Sewing machine

Straight pins

Thread: coordinating

Instructions

1. Cut two 8½" x 5"
rectangles from burlap.

2. Cut a 5" length from
linen ribbon. Fold top edge
of ribbon under ½" and press.

3. Using black textile ink,
center and stamp a chili
pepper onto ribbon. Allow
ink to dry.

4. Using textile markers,
color chili pepper red and
leaves green.

5. Center and pin ribbon to
top of one piece of burlap,
aligning bottom raw edges
together. Using a sewing
machine, top-stitch along
edges of ribbon.

6. Using a grommet tool
and following manufacturer's
instructions, center and
attach grommets ½" apart
and ¼" from top edge
of ribbon.

7. Place right sides of
burlap together. With a ½"
seam allowance, machine
stitch along sides and
bottom. Clip corners and,
using an iron, press
seams open.

8. Fold top edge of bag
under ¼" and press. Fold and
press again. Stitch close to
folded hem edge and turn
inside out.

9. Thread twine in large-
eyed needle and slip down
through one grommet and
burlap, around and up
through opposite side of
burlap and grommet. Pull
twine to gather bag and tie
into a bow.

10. Fold butcher paper in
half to form a triangle as
shown in Lemon & Chili Bags
Card Diagram on opposite
page. Unfold and fold in half
to form a rectangle. Unfold
and fold in half on opposite
side to form another
rectangle. Unfold and push
in sides so paper folds down
into a square gift tag.

11. Write desired message
or recipe on tag.

12. Cut string in half. Glue
a string to front and back of
tag. Glue corrugated squares
on front and back of folded
tag, covering string. Tie tag
to bag.

Chili Bag Placement

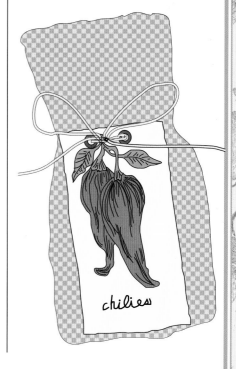

Vegetable Magnets Materials (for two)

Linen ribbon: 1⅜"-wide ivory (¼ yd.)

Magnetic sheet

Markers, textile: green, orange, red

Stamps, miniature: alphabet, artichoke, tomato

Textile ink: black

General Supplies & Tools

Tape: double-sided adhesive

Scissors: fabric; craft

Instructions

1. Using fabric scissors, cut a 3¼" and a 3½" length from linen ribbon.

2. Using black textile ink and 3¼" length of ribbon, center and stamp letters to spell "tomatoes". Re-ink stamp after each impression. Randomly stamp tomatoes around lettering. Allow ink to dry. Repeat process using remaining ribbon, letters to spell "artichoke", and artichoke stamp.

3. Using textile markers, color tomatoes orange and artichokes green. Randomly draw red "x's" around lettering and artichokes, and green dots around lettering and tomatoes.

4. Using craft scissors, cut a 1⅜" x 3¼" and a 1⅜" x 3½" rectangle from magnetic sheet. Apply double-sided adhesive tape to back side of ribbons and attach to magnetic squares.

Vegetable Magnets Placement

Checkerboard Magnets Materials (for three)

Linen ribbon: 2⅝"-wide black checkerboard (¼ yd.)

Magnetic sheet

Markers, textile: green,
   orange, red
Stamps, miniature:
   artichoke, tomato, turnip
Textile ink: black

General Supplies & Tools

Scissors: fabric, craft
Tape: double-sided adhesive

Instructions

1. Using fabric scissors, cut three 2½" lengths from black checkerboard ribbon.

2. Using black textile ink and one length of ribbon, stamp artichokes in ivory checkerboard squares. Re-ink stamp after each impression. Allow ink to dry. Repeat, using remaining ribbons and tomato and turnip stamps.

3. Using textile markers, color artichokes green, tomatoes orange, and turnips red.

4. Using craft scissors, cut three 2½" squares from magnetic sheet. Apply double-sided adhesive tape to back side of ribbons and attach to magnetic squares.

Checkerboard Magnets Placement

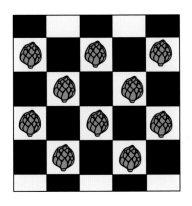  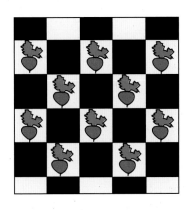

Green Pillow

Materials

Fabric: green (¼ yd.),
   green/black print (⅜ yd.)
Woven ribbon: 1½"-wide
   black (⅝ yd.)
Buttons, primitive: ¾"-½"
   coordinating (4)
Stamp: primitive diamond
Stuffing
Textile ink: black, green

General Supplies & Tools

Needles: hand-sewing
Scissors: fabric
Sewing machine
Straight pins
Thread: coordinating

Instructions

1. Cut two 11½" squares from green/black print fabric for pillow top and bottom.

2. Cut a 11½" x 5¾" rectangle from green fabric.

3. Using black textile ink, stamp three primitive diamonds, 1" apart, down center of green fabric.

4. Using green textile ink, stamp primitive diamonds onto black ribbon.

5. Cut black ribbon into two equal lengths. Pin ribbons to green fabric, ¾" from each edge of fabric. Using a sewing machine, top-stitch ribbons to fabric.

6. Fold long edges of green fabric under ¼". Pin green fabric to center of pillow top and top-stitch in place.

Materials

Cotton ribbon: 1½"-wide ivory (5½ yds.)
Box: 7¼" x 5¾" paper maché
Buttons: double-sided velcro
Charms: ¾" brass bee; ¼" flowers (6)
Markers, textile: green, pale orange, yellow
Rhinestones: yellow leaves (17)
Stamps: bee, leafless tree
Stationery, blank: 10¼" x 6¾", with matching envelopes (12)
Textile ink: black

General Supplies & Tools

Glue: craft
Scissors: fabric
Tape: double-sided adhesive

Instructions

1. Cut thirteen 1½" lengths from cotton ribbon for each piece of stationery and top of stationery box.

2. Using black textile ink, center and stamp bee on each ribbon square. Re-ink stamp after each impression. Allow ink to dry.

3. Using textile markers, color bee yellow and color wings yellow and green.

7. Sew buttons to pillow top, at ends and between stamped diamonds on green fabric as shown in Green Pillow Placement.

8. With right sides together and a ¼" seam, sew pillow top and bottom together, leaving an opening at one side for turning. Turn right side out and stuff pillow to desired firmness. Using a hand-sewing needle and coordinating thread, stitch opening closed.

Green Pillow Placement

8. Wrap ribbon around envelopes and glue at back of overlapping ribbon to secure.

9. Stamp tree onto left side of box lid. Allow ink to dry. Color tree trunk with pale orange textile marker.

10. Refer to Bee Stationery Placement below. Glue rhinestone leaves and brass flowers to branches of stamped tree. Glue brass bee charm to upper right corner of box lid. Glue stamped ribbon square to center bottom edge of box lid.

11. Fill box with stationery and envelopes.

4. Apply double-sided adhesive tape to backs of ribbons. Center and attach a stamped ribbon to top of each piece of stationery.

5. Fold stationery to 5½" x 6¾" notecards.

6. Repeat Steps 2 and 3 for back of envelope flaps.

7. From remaining ribbon, measure and cut a length of ribbon to wrap around envelopes, leaving a 1" overlap at back. Stamp ribbon and color with textile markers.

Bee Stationery Placement

Zebra Frame

Materials

Woven ribbon: 1½"-wide
  black (½ yd.), terra-cotta
  (½ yd.)
Buttons: 1" coordinating (4)
Mat board: 8" x 6¾" (2)
Sponges: applicator
Stamps: border tile, zebra
Stamping paint: black,
  terra-cotta

General Supplies & Tools

Glue gun and glue sticks
Knife: craft
Marker: black permanent
Paper plate
Ruler: metal straight edge
Scissors: fabric
Tape: double-sided adhesive

Instructions

1. Using fabric scissors, cut
two 6¾" lengths from black
ribbon.

2. Cut two 8" lengths from
terra-cotta ribbon.

3. Place ribbons as shown
in Zebra Frame Placement
on opposite page to
determine where images
should be stamped.

4. Pour a small amount of
each stamping paint onto
paper plate. Load flat edge
of applicator sponge with
black paint. Pat paint onto
zebra stamp. Stamp zebra on
terra-cotta ribbon. Repeat
process with border tile
stamp and terra-cotta paint.
Allow paint to dry.

5. Apply double-sided
adhesive tape to backs of
stamped ribbons. Attach
ribbons to mat board, first
placing the terra-cotta
ribbons at top and bottom of
frame and then black
ribbons to sides.

6. Using a metal ruler and
craft knife, carefully cut out
center of mat board.

7. Cut three ¾" x 4½"
spacers from center piece of

scrap mat board. Using a glue gun and glue sticks, hot-glue spacers to back side of ribbon-trimmed mat board at bottom and sides. Hot-glue remaining mat board over spacers.

8. Hot-glue buttons to corners of frame.

9. Using a black permanent marker, color edges of mat board.

10. Insert photo at top.

Zebra Frame Placement

Candlelight

Materials
Chiffon ribbon: 1"-wide white with gold edging (1 yd.)
Candle: 3" white
Embossing ink: clear
Embossing powder: gold
Stamp: double heart

General Supplies & Tools
Heat tool
Scissors: fabric

Instructions
1. Using embossing ink, stamp double hearts onto ribbon in desired pattern.

2. Apply embossing powder

over stamped pattern. Heat and allow to cool.
NOTE: when using heat tool, keep tool approximately 8" from ribbon to avoid scorching.

3. Wrap ribbon around candle and tie into a bow. Refer to General Instructions for Fork Cut on page 8. Fork-cut ends of ribbon.

Candlelight Placement

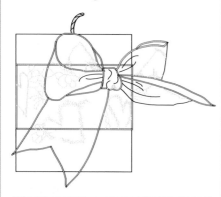

Gift Wrap

Materials
Chiffon ribbon: 1½"-wide white (2½ yds.)
Markers, metallic: green, purple
Stamp: leaf

General Supplies & Tools
Scissors: fabric

Instructions
1. Color stamp with metallic markers and stamp onto ribbon as desired.

2. Wrap ribbon around package and tie into a bow. Refer to General Instructions for Fork Cut on page 8. Fork-cut ends of ribbon.

Gift Wrap Placement

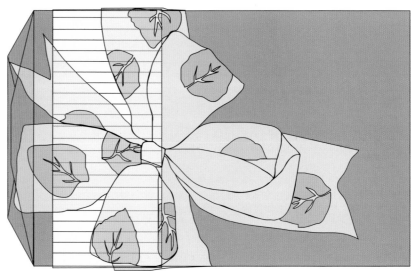

binding and punch holes as in Step 2.

4. Using dk. blue textile ink, randomly stamp buildings on pink ombré wire-edge ribbon and around top and bottom edge of journal cover.

5. Using alphabet stamps, stamp "My Journal" on top center of journal cover.

6. Thread ribbon through binding holes and tie into a bow. Refer to General Instructions for Fork Cut on page 8. Using fabric scissors, fork-cut ends of ribbon.

Sweet Home Journal Placement

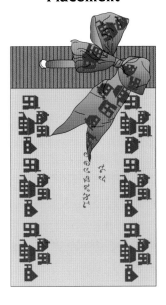

Materials
Wire-edge ribbon: 1½"-wide pink ombré (½ yd.)
Paper: ivory cardstock 8½" x 11" (6); brown corrugated 3⅛" x 5½"
Stamps: alphabet, small buildings
Textile ink: dk. blue

General Supplies & Tools
Paper punch
Scissors: craft, fabric

Instructions
1. Using craft scissors, cut ivory cardstock papers in half.

2. Punch two holes in left end of papers, ¼" from edge and 1" from top and bottom edges.

3. Cut brown corrugated paper to 5½" x 3¼". Evenly fold corrugated paper around left end of cardstock papers for

"emboss" over entire surface of fabric.

3. Color ivy stamp with green metallic pen and randomly stamp onto ribbon. Repeat process using grape stamp and purple metallic pen.

4. Wrap fabric around pillow. Fold raw edge under and, using a hand-sewing needle and coordinating thread, stitch seam closed.

5. Cut ribbon into two equal lengths. Wrap each ribbon around ends of pillow to gather fabric and tie into bows. Refer to General Instructions for Fork Cut on page 8. Fork-cut ends of ribbon.

Velvet Pillow Placement

Materials
Fabric: lt. green velvet (1 yd.)
Chiffon ribbon: 2"-wide green
  (1¾ yds.)
Markers, textile, metallic:
  green, purple
Pillow: 14" x 8" rectangle
Stamps: ivy, grape

General Supplies & Tools
Iron/ironing board
Needles: hand-sewing
Scissors: fabric

Spray bottle
Thread: coordinating

Instructions
1. Heat iron on high setting.

2. Lightly mist front and back of velvet fabric. Lay right side of fabric on top of clean ivy stamp and press with iron on wrong side of fabric until dry and impression is made. Randomly repeat to

Photo Albums

Materials

Linen ribbon: 2⅜"-wide ivory (3 yds.)
Acrylic paints: coordinating
Albums with pages
Braid: ⅛"-wide metallic gold (3 yds.)
Charms: brass bee (3)
Embossing powder: gold
Gesso
Pigment ink pads: brown, green, orange, dk. orange
Stamp: single leaf, leaf branch

Stamp pad: autumn rainbow
Thread: metallic gold

General Supplies & Tools

Brayer: rubber
Glue: craft
Heat tool
Needles: chenille, hand-sewing
Paintbrush
Scissors: fabric
Sewing machine

Album A Instructions

Refer to Album A Placement on page 59.

1. Measure and cut a length of linen ribbon to fit horizontally around album cover.

2. Using pigment ink pads, stamp leaf branches onto ribbon.

3. Randomly sprinkle gold embossing powder over stamped pattern. Heat and allow to cool.

4. Using a hand-sewing needle and metallic gold thread, tack bee charms to ribbon as desired.

5. Glue ribbon to outside cover, securing ends to inside of front and back covers.

Album B Instructions

Refer to Album B Placement on page 59.

1. Cut three 2¾" squares from linen ribbon.

2. Apply gesso to ribbons following manufacturer's instructions.

3. Paint ribbons in coordinating colors to match album cover. Let dry.

4. Using pigment ink, center and stamp single leaf on each ribbon. Apply embossing powder over stamped leaves. Heat and allow to cool.

5. Refer to General Instructions for Blanket Stitch on page 10. Using chenille needle and gold metallic braid, blanket-stitch around each ribbon.

6. Glue ribbons to album cover as desired.

Album C Instructions

Refer to Album C Placement on opposite page.

1. Measure and cut a length of linen ribbon to fit vertically around album cover.

2. Roll brayer in autumn rainbow stamp pad. Roll brayer on ribbon in a variety of directions.

3. Using pigment ink pads, stamp single leaves onto ribbon. Randomly apply embossing powder over a few stamped leaves and sprinkle in various spots

on ribbon. Heat and allow to cool.

4. Glue ribbon to outside cover, securing ends to inside of front and back covers.

Photo Page A Instructions

Refer to Photo Page A Placement on opposite page.

1. Cut two 3½" lengths from linen ribbon.

2. Roll brayer in autumn rainbow stamp pad. Roll brayer on ribbons in a variety of directions.

3. Using pigment ink pads, stamp single leaves onto ribbons.

4. Lay ribbons side by side, slightly overlapping. Using metallic gold thread and sewing machine, sew ribbons together and around outside edges with a zig zag stitch.

5. Glue sides and bottom of ribbon to photo page for a pocket.

6. Cut an 8" length of linen ribbon.

7. Using autumn rainbow stamp pad, stamp four leaf branches onto ribbon. Randomly sprinkle

embossing powder over stamped leaves. Heat and allow to cool.

8. Using fabric scissors, cut out stamped leaves and use as corner photo mounts on photo pages.

Photo Page B Instructions

Refer to Photo Page B Placement on opposite page.

1. Cut two 24" lengths and one 4½" x 1" strip from linen ribbon.

2. Roll brayer in autumn rainbow stamp pad. Roll brayer on ribbons in a variety of directions.

3. Lay 24" ribbons side by side, slightly overlapping. Using metallic gold thread and sewing machine, sew ribbons together and around outside edges with a zig zag stitch.

4. Fold ribbon into an envelope as shown. Using autumn rainbow stamp pad, stamp single leaves onto envelope and ribbon strip.

5. Stamp a single leaf onto a scrap of linen ribbon. Apply embossing powder over stamped leaf. Heat and allow to cool.

6. Cut out leaf and glue to center edge of envelope flap.

7. Glue envelope to photo page.

8. Glue ribbon strip to photo page to use as photo mount.

Album C Placement

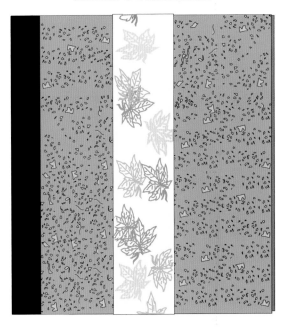

Album A Placement

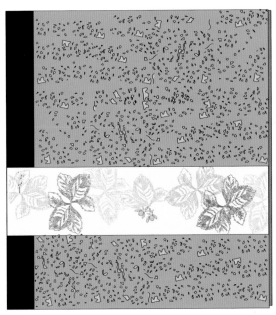

Album B Placement

Photo Page A Placement

Photo Page B Placement

thoughts" in staggered rows, a few rows at a time, across muslin fabric. Re-ink stamp after each impression.

2. After stamping a few rows, randomly apply clear and silver embossing powder over stamped pattern. Heat and allow to cool. Repeat.

3. Using fabric scissors, cut a 6" length from linen ribbon. Using purple textile ink, stamp vase ¾" above bottom edge of ribbon.

4. Using a pencil, trace topiary Ribbon Topiary Transfer Pattern on opposite page onto a piece of tracing paper. Tape tracing paper onto a sun-lit window and tape stamped ribbon in place over design. Using a disappearing pen, trace design onto ribbon.

5. Refer to General Instructions for Embroidery Stitches on pages 10-12. Using embroidery and chenille needles, embroider topiary design following Topiary Stitch Guide on opposite page.

Materials

Fabric: 9½" square tan muslin

Embroidery ribbon: 4mm lt. blue, gold, green, lavender, yellow (1 yd. each); 7mm pink (1 yd.)

Linen ribbon: 2½"-wide ivory (¼ yd.)

Embossing powder: clear, silver

Stamps: "You are in my thoughts", vase

Textile ink: burgundy, purple

Tracing paper

General Supplies & Tools

Glue: craft

Heat tool

Needles: chenille, embroidery

Pencil

Pen: disappearing

Scissors: fabric

Tape

Instructions

1. Using burgundy textile ink, stamp "You are in my

6. Fold top and bottom edge of ribbon under ½" and glue to secure.

7. Center and glue embroidered ribbon onto left side of fabric. Frame as desired.

Ribbon Topiary Stitch Guide

	Description	Ribbon	Stitch
1.	Buds	4mm yellow	French Knot
2.	Buds	4mm lt. blue	French Knot
3.	Leaves	4mm green	Lazy Daisy Stitch
4.	Roses	7mm pink	Folded Rose
5.	Violets	4mm lavender	Free Form Flower
6.	Stem	4mm gold	Stem Stitch

Ribbon Topiary Transfer Pattern Enlarge 115%

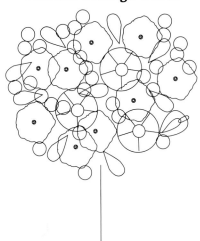

Ribbon Topiary Stitch Guide

Ribbon Topiary Placement

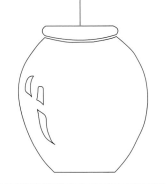

Ribbon Quilt

Note: Because this project uses pigment ink, it is designed for decorative purposes only.

Materials
Linen ribbon: width and amount to be determined by size and color of quilt
Sheer ribbon: width and amount to be determined by size and color of quilt
Embossing powder: clear
Pigment ink pads: coordinating colors
Stamps: coordinating

General Supplies & Tools
Heat tool
Scissors: fabric

Instructions
1. Using one color of pigment ink, stamp linen ribbon with desired stamp and in desired pattern. Re-ink stamp after each impression. Allow ink to dry.

2. Choose a different stamp and ink color. Stamp sheer

Materials

Linen ribbon: 1½"-wide ivory
   (2¾ yds.)
Acrylic paints: dk. brown,
   burgundy, purple, silver
Desk set
Embossing powders:
   burgundy, clear, metallic
   gold
Gesso
Stamps: hearts, stars
Textile ink: gold, silver

General Supplies & Tools

Glue: craft
Heat tool
Paintbrushes
Scissors: fabric

Instructions

1. Measure and cut ribbon
to fit individual pieces of
desk accessories.

2. To create a surface
similar to canvas, apply
gesso to each ribbon using
smooth even brush strokes
and following manufacturer's
instructions.

3. Paint each gesso-treated
ribbon with desired patterns,
alternating and combining
colors using a variety of
painting techniques. Let dry.

ribbon in
desired pattern.

3. Apply clear
embossing powder over
stamped pattern. Heat
and allow to cool.
NOTE: when using heat
tool, keep tool
approximately 8"
from ribbon to
avoid scorching.

4. Lay sheer ribbon on
top of linen ribbon.
Sew ribbons to border
of quilt or to desired
location on quilt.

Ribbon Quilt Placement

4. Using textile inks, stamp hearts and stars onto ribbons in desired pattern. Apply desired embossing powders over stamped pattern on ribbons. Heat and allow to cool.

5. Glue ribbons to desk accessories using Desk Set Placement below and on following page as a general guide.

Desk Set Placement (Small Note Box & Pencil Box—Front View & Side View)

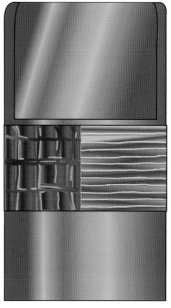

Desk Set Placement (Large Note Box)

Oriental Pillows

Materials
Ribbon: coordinating, in
    desired width (½ yd. for
    each)
Embossing powder: copper
Pillows: 12" x 4"-diameter
    bolster (2)
Stamps: leaf vine, swirl
Textile ink: black

General Supplies & Tools
Heat tool
Needles: hand-sewing
Scissors: fabric
Thread: coordinating

Instructions
1. Measure and cut two

pieces of ribbon to fit around each pillow at both ends.

2. Using black textile ink, randomly stamp leaf vines to first set of ribbons for one pillow and swirls onto second set of ribbons for the second pillow.

3. Randomly sprinkle copper embossing powder over stamped patterns on first set of ribbons and cover entire stamped pattern on second set of ribbons. Heat and allow to cool.

4. Refer to Oriental Pillows Placement. Using a hand-sewing needle and coordinating thread, tack each set of ribbons to each pillow.

Oriental Pillows Placement

Picture Hanger

Materials
Burlap ribbon: 1½"-wide ivory (⅞ yd.)
Embossing powder: clear, gold metallic
Stamps: primitive (5); sand
Stamp pads: autumn rainbow, black

General Supplies & Tools
Brayer: rubber
Heat tool

Instructions
1. Roll brayer in autumn rainbow stamp pad. Roll brayer on ribbon in a variety of directions.

2. Using autumn rainbow stamp pad, stamp primitive designs onto ribbon in desired pattern.

3. Apply clear embossing powder over stamped pattern. Heat and cool.

4. Using black stamp pad, randomly stamp sand designs onto ribbon. Apply gold metallic embossing powder over stamped pattern and in random tiny specks across the ribbon. Heat and allow to cool.

5. Attach to desired picture.

Very Cherry

Cherry Placemat
Materials
Fabric: red burlap (½ yd.)
Cotton ribbon: 1½"-wide
  (2 yds.)
Sponges: wedge (2)
Stamp: cherry
Textile ink: green, red

General Supplies & Tools
Iron/ironing board
Scissors: craft; fabric
Sewing machine
Thread: coordinating

Instructions
1. Using fabric scissors, cut burlap into a 14" x 20" rectangle.

2. Cut two 14" lengths and two 20" lengths from cotton ribbon.

3. Fold ribbon ends under ½" and press. Lay ribbons on burlap as shown in photo to determine placement for stamped images.

4. Calculate number and placement of cherries on ribbon by stamping several images on scrap paper. Using craft scissors, cut out images and space proportionately along length of ribbons as desired.

Picture Hanger Placement

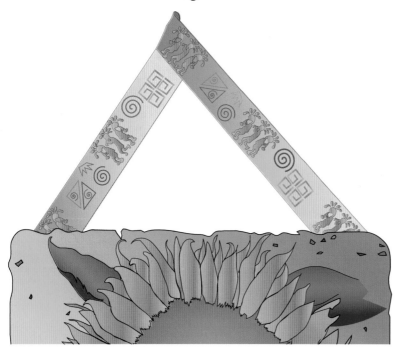

66

Cherry Hatbox

Materials

Cotton ribbon: 1½"-wide ivory (¾ yd.); 2⅝"-wide black/white checkerboard (¾ yd.)

Grosgrain ribbon: ½"-wide red (1½ yds.)

Acrylic paints: ivory, red

Hatbox: 8"-diameter paper maché

Sponges: wedge (2)

Stamp: cherry

Textile inks: green, red

General Supplies & Tools

Paintbrush

Scissors: craft; fabric

Tape: double-sided adhesive

Instructions

1. Paint hatbox lid using ivory acrylic paint. Paint bottom of hatbox using red acrylic paint.

2. Using fabric scissors, measure and cut ivory cotton ribbon to fit around circumference of hatbox, allowing a ½" overlap.

3. Calculate number and placement of cherries on ribbon by stamping several images on scrap paper. Using craft scissors, cut out images and space proportionately along length of ribbon as desired.

5. Apply red textile ink to a wedge sponge and ink appropriate portion of cherry stamp. Repeat process using green textile ink. Remove paper images and stamp ribbon. Re-apply inks after each impression.

6. Sew ribbons around border of placemat. Fray edges of burlap.

Cherry Placemat Placement

4. Apply red textile ink to flat edge of wedge sponge and ink appropriate portion of cherry stamp. Repeat process using green textile ink. Remove paper images and stamp ribbon. Re-apply inks after each impression.

5. Following process in Step 4, randomly stamp top of hatbox lid.

6. Apply double-sided adhesive tape to back of stamped ribbon.

7. Using fabric scissors, measure and cut red grosgrain ribbon into two lengths to create a border on both sides of stamped ribbon. Adhere grosgrain ribbon to back of stamped ribbon.

8. Center and attach stamped ribbon to checkerboard ribbon. Apply double-sided adhesive tape to back of checkerboard ribbon. Attach checkerboard ribbon around hatbox, overlapping ends ½".

Cherry Hatbox Placement

Fern Journal

Materials

Cotton ribbon: 2"-wide ivory/tan striped (¾ yd.)
Grommet: green
Journal: 4¼" x 6¼"
Paper: green handmade (1 sheet)
Stamp: fern
Textile ink: green
Twine (1 yd.)

General Supplies & Tools

Glue gun and glue sticks
Grommet tool
Scissors: craft; fabric
Tape: double-sided adhesive

Instructions

1. Using craft scissors, measure and cut handmade paper to fit top of journal. Apply double-sided adhesive tape to back of paper and attach to top of journal cover.

2. Using fabric scissors, measure and cut a vertical length of ribbon to fit top of journal cover.

3. Using green textile ink, stamp fern onto ribbon. Re-ink stamp after each impression. Allow ink to dry.

Fern Journal Placement

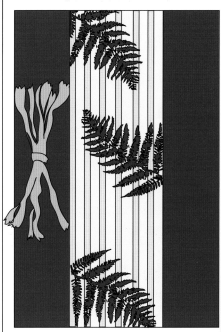

Fern Journal Bookmark Placement

4. Apply double-sided adhesive tape to back of stamped ribbon. Center and attach ribbon to top of journal cover.

5. Cut a 4" length from twine. Tie a knot in center of twine and fray ends to create a bow. Using a glue gun and glue sticks, attach twine bow to left center edge of journal cover.

6. Cut a 16" length from ribbon. Stamp ribbon as in Step 3.

7. Apply double-sided adhesive tape to back of ribbon. Fold ribbon in half, wrong sides together, to form bookmark.

8. Using a grommet tool, attach grommet to center top of folded ribbon.

9. Thread remaining twine through grommet and tie a knot at top of bookmark and at ends of twine.

Checked Hearts Towel

2. Remove paper images and, using black textile ink, stamp hearts onto ribbon. Re-ink stamp after each impression. Allow ink to dry. Using red textile marker, color in hearts as desired.

3. Cut red grosgrain ribbon in half. Fold ends under ¼" and, using iron, press. Fold ends of stamped ribbon under ¼". Pin grosgrain ribbon to backside edges of stamped ribbon to create a border.

4. Lay ribbon on hand-towel, ½" from bottom edge. Sew along inside edges of stamped ribbon to attach ribbon to hand towel.

Materials

Cotton ribbon: 1⅜"-wide white (½ yd.)

Grosgrain ribbon: ½"-wide red (1 yd.)

Hand towel, premade: blue/white checked

Marker, textile: red

Stamp: checkerboard heart

Textile ink: black

General Supplies & Tools

Iron/ironing board

Scissors: craft; fabric
Sewing machine
Thread: coordinating

Instructions

1. Calculate number and placement of hearts on white cotton ribbon by stamping several images on scrap paper. Using craft scissors, cut out images and space proportionately along length of ribbon as desired.

Checked Hearts Towel Placement

Sunflower Journal

3. Using textile markers, color sunflowers on journal cover and ribbon.

4. Cut a 6½" x 2½" length from green fabric. Slightly fray edges.

5. Apply double-sided adhesive tape to back of stamped ribbon. Center and attach ribbon to green fabric strip.

6. Fold ends of fabric strip under ¼". Apply double-sided adhesive tape to back of fabric strip. Attach fabric strip to left side of journal cover.

Materials
Woven ribbon: 1½"-wide
　white (¼ yd.)
Fabric scrap: green
Journal, blank: 6" square
Markers, textile: green,
　orange, yellow
Stamp: sunflower
Textile ink: black

General Supplies & Tools
Scissors: fabric
Tape: double-sided adhesive

Instructions
1. Using black textile ink, randomly stamp sunflowers on front cover of journal. Re-ink stamp after each impression. Allow ink to dry.

2. Cut a 6½" length from woven ribbon. Stamp ribbon with sunflowers. Allow ink to dry.

Sunflower Journal Placement

Ann Snuggs

Childhood visits to her great-great grandfather's floral nursery and the many wonderful sensory experiences that took place there have been the creative influences in Ann Snugg's designing career. Memories of garden parties, linens, laces, birthday cakes embellished with fresh flowers, and joyful walks down the meandering azalea-lined drive are the inspiration for her creative endeavors. Knowing that she wanted to be in the art field, Ann first sought a degree in commercial art from Limestone College in South Carolina. She was quickly drawn back to her beginnings, though, and switched to the American Floral Art School in Chicago, and also attended the Benz School of Floral Design in Houston.

As a lifelong embroidery and horticultural enthusiast, Ann began designing ribbon embroidery and incorporating her exquisite pressed flowers into her designs in 1993. This delightful combination of talents has been featured in both needlework and craft magazines. Ann would like to thank her husband Joe for his patience.

Embroidery hoop
Glue: craft
Iron/ironing board
Needles: chenille; embroidery;
    #10 sharp
Scissors: craft; fabric
Tape: masking
Thread: extra fine
Toothpicks
Tweezers

Instructions

1. Refer to Color Copy
Pattern on following page.
Make color copy on standard
copy or card stock paper at
copy center.

2. Using #10 sharp needle
and extra fine thread, fold
fabric edges under and baste
to prevent fraying.

3. Refer to General
Instructions for Transferring
on page 15. Enlarge Bird
Bath Transfer Pattern on
page 75. Center and transfer
design onto fabric.

4. Place fabric tightly in
embroidery hoop.

5. Refer to General
Instructions for Embroidery
Stitches on pages 10-12.

Materials

Fabric: 11" x 14" white
    Monaco (28 count)
Embroidery ribbon: 2mm
    burgundy, lavender,
    dk. pink (7 yds. each);
    4mm cream, olive
    green, lt. olive green,
    mauve, dk. yellow (5 yds.
    of each); 7mm soft pink
    (3 yds.)
Embroidery floss: dk. green,
    lt. green, lavender, yellow

Mat board: 11" x 14" precut
    lt. mauve
Paper: copy or card stock
Pressed flowers: small
    blue hydrangea, Queen
    Anne's lace, blue verbena,
    purple alyssum, daisies,
    moss, spirea, yellow
    wildflower, large bright
pink verbena

General Supplies & Tools

Cloth: soft, white

Using embroidery and chenille needles, embroider flower garden following Bird Bath Stitch Guide on page 76.

6. After embroidering, use #10 sharp needle and thread to tack all ribbon ends to back of fabric.

7. Remove fabric from embroidery hoop. Place front side down on soft, white cloth and press with iron.

8. Using fabric scissors, cut fabric to 9" x 12", making certain embroidered flower garden is centered. Center embroidered flower garden in precut lt. mauve mat opening. Using masking tape, tape fabric to back of mat.

9. Using craft scissors, cut out color-copied paper bird bath and each individual rock path piece. Using craft glue, attach bird bath and rock path pieces to fabric. Refer to Bird Bath Transfer Pattern. Let glue dry.

10. Using tweezers, place pressed flowers on embroidered flower garden. Refer to Bird Bath Flower Placement diagram on opposite page for placement. Using toothpick and a small amount of craft glue, dab glue on center back of each flower and gently press in place.

11. Make butterfly by placing two small blue

verbena petals on each side of a small stem piece of yellow wildflower. Glue in place. Glue moss around and in-between rock path pieces.

12. Frame as desired.

Color Copy Pattern   Enlarge 110%

Bird Bath Transfer Pattern/Flower Placement   Enlarge 220%

Bird Bath Flower Placement

A. Queen Anne's Lace
B. Pink Verbena
C. Purple Alyssum
D. Spirea
E. Daisy
F. Yellow Wildflower
G. Blue Verbena
H. Blue Hydrangea
I. Moss

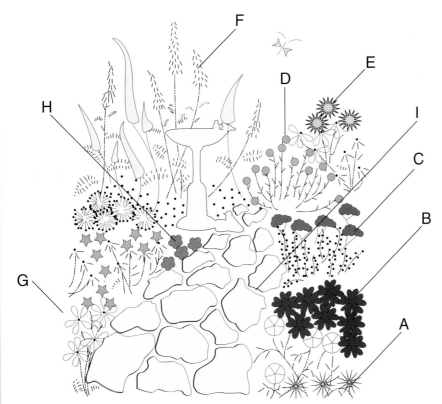

Bird Bath Picture Placement

Bird Bath Stitch Guide

Description	Ribbon	Stitch
1. Rose Centers	cream	Spider Web Rose
2. Rose Petals	soft pink	Spider Web Rose
3. Rose Bud	soft pink	Straight Stitch
4. Stems	lt. green floss (2 strands)	Stem Stitch
5. Leaves	lt. olive green	Straight Stitch
6. Flowers	lavender	French Knot
7. Stems	lavender floss (2 strands)	Stem Stitch
8. Flower Petals	soft pink	Straight Stitch
9. Flower Centers	mauve	Straight Stitch
10. Stems	dk. green floss (2 strands)	Stem Stitch
11. Leaves	olive green	Straight Stitch
12. Flower Petals	burgundy	Lazy Daisy Stitch
13. Flower Centers	dk. yellow	French Knot
14. Stems	lt. green floss (2 strands)	Stem Stitch
15. Stems	lt. green floss (2 strands)	Stem Stitch
16. Flowers	dk. pink	Straight Stitch
17. Stems	dk. green floss (2 strands)	Stem Stitch
18. Leaves	olive green	Satin Stitch
19. Flowers	cream	French Knot
20. Flowers	dk. yellow	French Knot
21. Flower Petals	mauve	Japanese Ribbon Stitch
22. Flower Centers	yellow floss (1 strand)	French Knot and Straight Stitch
23. Flower Petals	cream	Straight Stitch
24. Flower Centers	lt. olive green	Stem Stitch
25. Flower Petals	soft pink	Straight Stitch
26. Flower Centers	mauve	Straight Stitch
27. Flower Petals	burgundy	Lazy Daisy Stitch
28. Flower Centers	dk. yellow	French Knot
29. Stems	dk. green floss (2 strands)	Stem Stitch
30. Leaves	olive green	Satin Stitch

Bird Bath Stitch Guide

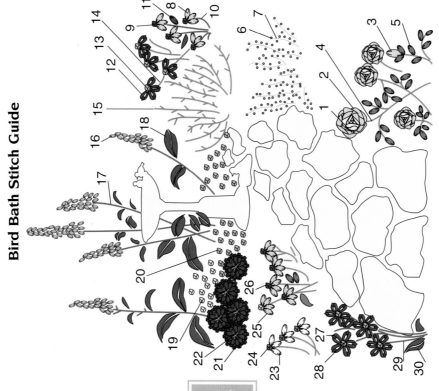

embroidery; #10 sharp
Paper: tracing
Pencil
Ruler
Scissors: craft; fabric
Straight pins
Thread: extra fine
Toothpicks
Tweezers

Instructions

1. Using #10 sharp needle and extra fine thread, stitch around edge of fabric to prevent fraying.

2. Refer to General Instructions for Transferring on page 15. Using Initial Transfer Pattern on page 79, enlarge inner oval. Center and transfer oval onto fabric.

3. Select and enlarge initial from pages 80-81. Center and transfer initial design inside oval onto fabric.

4. Place fabric tightly in embroidery hoop.

5. Refer to General Instructions for Embroidery Stitches on pages 10-12. Using embroidery and chenille needles, embroider

Materials

Fabric: 12" x 15" lavender Damask

Embroidery ribbon: 4mm mauve, lavender (10 yds. each); 7mm lavender (6 yds.)

Embroidery floss: green, lavender

Pressed flowers: bachelor button petals, rabbit's foot fern, purple Johnny-jump-ups, Queen Anne's lace, lobelia, yellow marigolds, lavender phlox, spirea, pink verbena

Foam core board: 11" x 14" white

Fleece: lightweight (½ yd.)

General Supplies & Tools

Embroidery hoop
Glue: craft
Iron/ironing board
Needles: chenille;

initial and oval border. Follow Initial Stitch Guide on opposite page.

6. Remove fabric from embroidery hoop and place front side down on work table.

7. Using fabric scissors, cut fleece into one 6½" x 8½" piece and one 11" x 14" piece.

8. Using tracing paper, pencil and craft scissors, trace and cut out enlarged inner oval pattern. Trace oval pattern onto smaller fleece piece.

9. Using fabric scissors, cut out oval from fleece. Lay oval fleece piece on back center of design. Lay larger fleece piece over oval fleece piece. Turn design over and match edges of quilt batting with fabric. Using straight pins, secure in place.

10. Using #10 sharp needle and extra fine thread, tack initial and oval border to fleece.

11. Press 4mm lavender embroidery ribbon with iron. Using ruler and dots on fabric as guide, diagonally in two directions lay pieces of 4mm lavender embroidery ribbon

to form diamonds. Diamonds should be approximately 1¼". Cut and pin ribbon in place at ends.

12. Baste edges of fabric and fleece together.

13. Using embroidery needle and mauve embroidery ribbon, tack ribbons at cross sections with a straight stitch.

14. Using #10 sharp needle and extra fine thread, tack ribbon ends to fabric to securely hold in place.

15. Center and pin embroidered fabric onto foam core.

16. Using embroidery needle and two strands of lavender embroidery floss, stitch oval border again and outer edge of design through foam core. Trim excess fabric and fleece from edges of foam core.

17. Using tweezers, place pressed flowers on design. Refer to photograph on previous page or Initial Placement.

18. Using toothpick and a small amount of craft glue, dab glue on center back of each flower and gently press in place as desired. Let glue dry.

19. Frame as desired.

Initial Placement

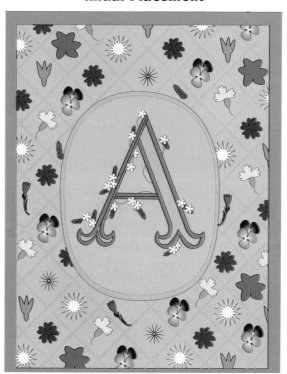

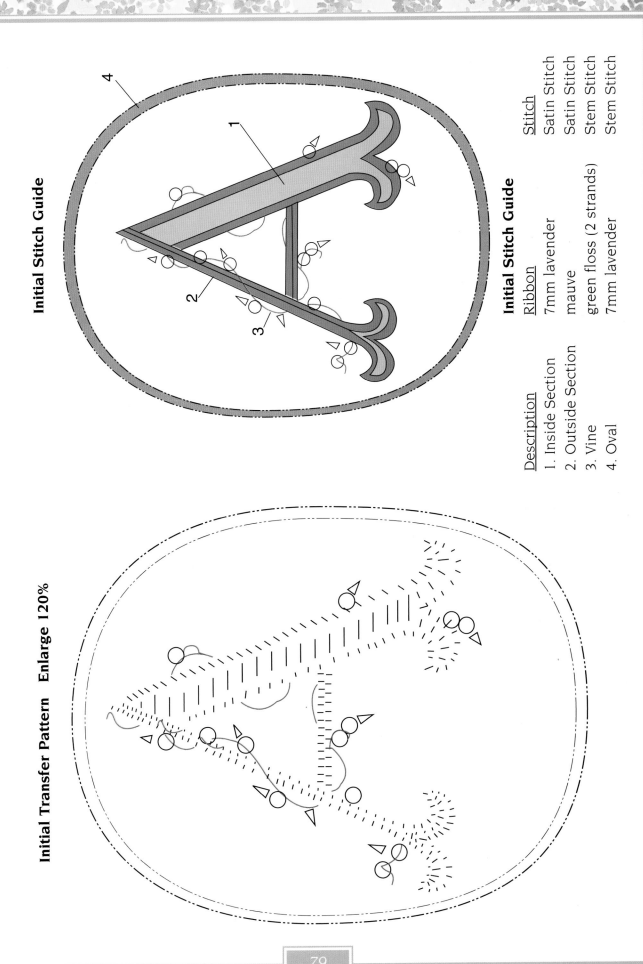

Initial Stitch Guide

Initial Stitch Guide

Description	Ribbon	Stitch
1. Inside Section	7mm lavender	Satin Stitch
2. Outside Section	mauve	Satin Stitch
3. Vine	green floss (2 strands)	Stem Stitch
4. Oval	7mm lavender	Stem Stitch

Initial Transfer Pattern   Enlarge 120%

B C D

E F G

H I J K

L M N

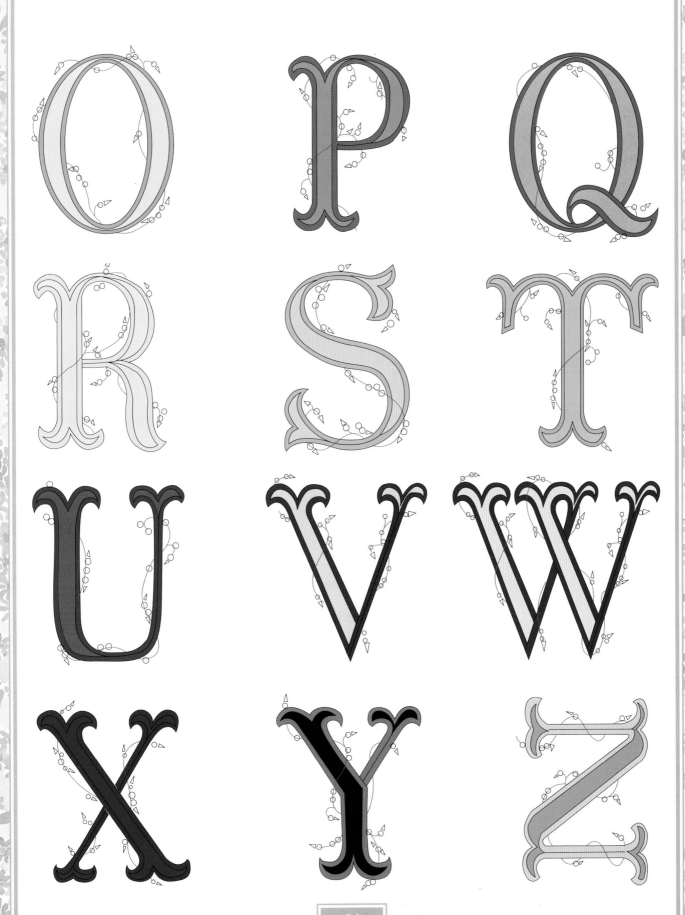

Potted Salvia

Copy Pattern on opposite page on standard copy or card stock paper at copy center.

2. Using craft scissors, cut out color-copied clay pot.

3. Using #10 sharp needle and extra fine thread, stitch around edge of fabric to prevent fraying.

4. Refer to General Instructions for Transferring on page 15. Use Potted Salvia Transfer Pattern on opposite page to center and transfer design to fabric.

5. Place fabric tightly in embroidery hoop.

6. Refer to General Instructions for Embroidery Stitches on pages 10-12. Using embroidery needle, embroider flower design following Potted Salvia Stitch Guide on opposite page.

7. Remove fabric from embroidery hoop. Place front side down on soft, white cloth and press.

Materials

Fabric: 7" x 8" beige Monaco (28 count)
Embroidery ribbon: 4mm ivory, olive green, lavender, (5 yds. each)
Embroidery floss: green
Mat board: 5" x 7" precut dk. green
Dried moss

Embroidery hoop
Glue: craft
Iron/ironing board
Needles: embroidery; #10 sharp
Scissors: craft
Tape: masking
Thread: extra fine
Toothpicks
Tweezers

General Supplies & Tools

Cloth: soft, white

Instructions

1. Make color copy of Color

8. Center flower design on dk. green pre-cut mat. Using masking tape, attach fabric to back of mat.

9. Using craft glue, attach clay pot to fabric, following Potted Salvia Placement.

10. Using toothpick, dab a small amount of craft glue on back of moss. Using tweezers, place moss on top of clay pot and gently press in place. Let glue dry.

11. Frame as desired.

Color Copy Pattern

Potted Salvia Transfer Pattern

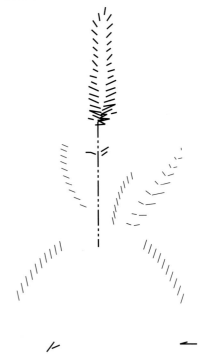

Potted Salvia Stitch Guide

Description	Ribbon	Stitch
1. Leaves	olive green	Satin Stitch
2. Stem	green floss (4 strands)	Stem Stitch
3. Flower Petals	lavender	Straight Stitch
4. Flower Petals	ivory	Straight Stitch

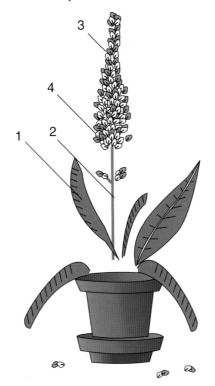

Potted Salvia Placement

Flower Basket

Instructions

1. Using dk. brown ink pad and basket rubber stamp, stamp basket design onto brown paper bag. Using craft scissors, cut out basket.

2. Using craft knife, cut slits on each side of bottom portion of basket center, having one slit slightly higher than other slit. Refer to Flower Basket Transfer Pattern opposite page.

3. Using fabric scissors, cut three small pieces of burgundy embroidery ribbon. Weave one ribbon through slits. Using craft glue, secure ribbon ends to back of basket. Glue remaining two ribbons to upper portion of basket handle, at a slight diagonal. Turn ends under basket handle and glue.

4. Using fabric glue, center and glue basket to fabric. Let glue dry.

5. Using masking tape, attach fabric to back of precut dk. green mat. Refer to General Instructions for Transferring on page 15.

Materials

Fabric: 7" x 9" beige Monaco (28 count)

Embroidery ribbon: 2mm olive green (7 yds.); 4mm blue, burgundy, mauve, yellow (5 yds. each)

Brown paper bag: small

Ink pad: dk. brown

Rubber stamp: 3" basket

Mat board: 8" x 10" precut dk. green

Pressed flowers: daisies, blue hydrangea, purple Johnny-jump-ups, leaves, blue salvia, spirea, yellow wildflower

General Supplies & Tools

Glue: craft; fabric

Knife: craft

Needles: embroidery

Scissors: craft; fabric

Tape: masking

Toothpicks

Tweezers

Transfer Flower Basket Transfer Pattern to fabric.

6. Refer to General Instructions for Embroidery Stitches on pages 10-12. Using embroidery needle, embroider flower design, following Flower Basket Stitch Guide.

7. Refer to Flower Basket Placement on following page. Using tweezers, place pressed flowers on embroidered flower basket design.

8. Using toothpick and a small amount of craft glue, dab glue on center back of each flower and gently press in place. Let glue dry.

9. Frame as desired.

Flower Basket Transfer Pattern   Enlarge 125%

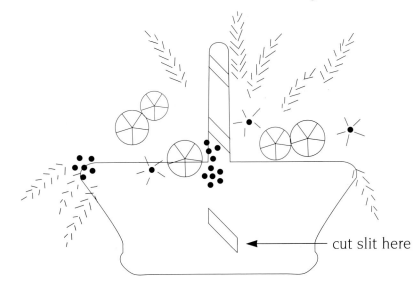

cut slit here

Flower Basket Stitch Guide

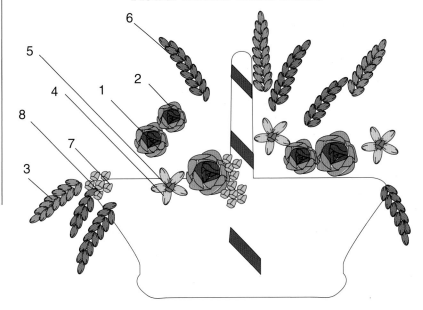

Flower Basket Stitch Guide

Description	Ribbon	Stitch
1. Rose Centers	burgundy	Spider Web Rose
2. Rose Petals	mauve	Spider Web Rose
3. Snapdragon	mauve	Straight Stitch
4. Daisy Petals	yellow	Padded Straight Stitch
5. Daisy Centers	olive green	1-Wrap French Knot
6. Leaves	olive green	Straight Stitch
7. Forget-Me-Not Petals	blue	1-Wrap French Knot
8. Forget-Me-Not Centers	yellow	1-Wrap French Knot

Flower Basket Placement

Materials

Fabric: 29" x 13" cream
   Belfast linen (22 count)
Embroidery ribbon: 2mm
   olive green (7 yds.);
   4mm dk. pink (11½ yds.);
   7mm lavender (15 yds.)
Embroidery floss: dk. pink
Pressed flowers: daisy, fern,
   purple Johnny-Jump-Ups,
   lavender larkspur, lobelia,
   spirea, pink verbena,
   yellow wildflower
Foam core board: 25" x 9"
   white

General Supplies & Tools

Cloth: soft, white
Glue: craft
Iron/ironing board
Needles: chenille;
   embroidery; #10 sharp
Scissors
Straight pins
Tape: masking
Thread: extra fine
Toothpicks
Tweezers

Instructions

1. Using #10 sharp needle
and extra fine thread, stitch
around fabric to prevent
fraying.

2. Refer to General

Instructions for Transferring
on page 15. Enlarge
Welcome Transfer Pattern on
page 88. Center and transfer
design onto fabric.

3. Refer to General
Instructions for Embroidery
Stitches on pages 10-12.
Using embroidery and
chenille needles, embroider
welcome design following
Welcome Stitch Guides on
opposite page.

4. Place front side down on
soft, white cloth and press
with iron.

5. Center design onto foam

core. Secure fabric to foam core by sticking pins straight into edge of lavender border about an inch apart.

6. Fold and glue excess fabric to back of foam core and secure with masking tape. Remove pins from lavender border.

7. Using tweezers, place pressed flowers on embroidered welcome design. Refer to Welcome Placement on following page.

8. Using toothpick and a small amount of craft glue, dab glue on center back of each flower and gently press in place. Do not put glue on flower petals. Let glue dry.

9. Frame as desired.

Welcome Stitch Guide

Description	Ribbon	Stitch
1. Wide Letter Sections	dk. pink	Satin Stitch
2. Narrow Letter Sections	dk. pink floss (2 strands)	Stem Stitch
3. Border	lavender	Satin Stitch
(Place stitches closely together so border appears gathered.)		
4. Vines	olive green	Stem Stitch

Welcome Transfer Pattern & Flower Placement Enlarge 240%

Welcome Placement

Dogwood Pillow

Materials

Fabric: 16" x 16" green, linen (2)

Mesh ribbon: 3⅛"-wide gold wired (3 yds.)

Embroidery ribbon: 4mm olive green (5 yds.); 7mm lt. green (6 yds.), ivory (27 yds.)

Embroidery floss: brown, green

Embroidery thread: lt. gold metallic

Pillow form: 14" x 14"

Quilt batting: 15" x 15" lightweight (2)

Trim: ⅛"-wide gold braided (1 yd.)

General Supplies & Tools

Embroidery hoop

Iron/ironing board

Needles: chenille; embroidery; hand-sewing

Fabric marker: disappearing

Ruler

Scissors: fabric

Sewing machine

Straight pins

Thread: coordinating

Instructions

1. Pull threads to square up each piece of linen fabric.

2. Using hand-sewing needle and coordinating thread, stitch around fabric to prevent fraying.

3. Refer to General Instructions for Transferring on page 15. Enlarge Dogwood Pillow Transfer Pattern on following page. Center and transfer design onto center of one linen fabric piece.

4. Using ruler and fabric marker, center and mark an 8"-square around embroidery pillow pattern.

5. Place linen fabric tightly in embroidery hoop.

6. Refer to General Instructions for Embroidery Stitches on pages 10-12. Using embroidery and chenille needles, embroider flower design following

Dogwood Pillow Stitch Guides on opposite page.

7. Using hand-sewing needle and gold embroidery thread, sew gold braided trim onto 8" square.

8. Place front side down on soft, white cloth and press with iron.

9. Place embroidered fabric on top of one quilt batting square. Randomly tack fabric to quilt batting within embroidered design. Using gold thread, tack fabric to quilt batting through gold braid.

10. Baste fabric along outside edges. Baste remaining fabric piece and quilt batting square together at outside edges.

11. Using straight pins and with right sides together, pin fabric pieces together. Using sewing machine, sew fabric pieces together with ½" seam allowance. Leave an 8" opening to turn. Clip seam.

12. Turn fabric right side out and insert pillow form. Stitch opening closed.

13. To make ruffle, fold gold mesh ribbon in half

lengthwise. Fold again, ½" up from first fold. Pin to hold.

14. Use fingers to bunch ribbon together at second fold, creating a ruffle.

15. Using gold embroidery thread, hand-sew ruffle around pillow edge. Where ribbon ends meet, seam together.

16. Shape ruffle to desired fullness by stretching layers of ribbon outward. Stretch bottom layer 2". Stretch middle layer 1½" and stretch top layer 1".

Dogwood Pillow Transfer Pattern   Enlarge 165%

Dogwood Pillow Stitch Guide

Description	Ribbon	Stitch
1. Flower Petal Section	ivory	Straight Stitch
2. Flower Centers	olive green	2-Wrap French Knot
3. Leaf Sections	lt. green	Straight Stitch
4. Petal Outline	green floss (3 strands)	Stem Stitch
5. Petal Indentations	brown floss (6 strands)	Padded Satin Stitch

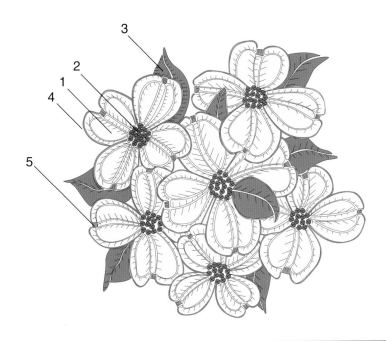

Dogwood Pillow Placement

Heart Note Card

Materials

Fabric: 6" x 6" cream
 Hardanger (22 count)
Note card: 5" x 6½" cream
 with gold trim and
 matching envelope
Embroidery ribbon: 4mm
 blue, olive green, ivory,
 mauve, soft pink, yellow
 (5 yds. each)
Embroidery floss: pink
Trim: ⅛"-wide gold braided
 (½ yd.)

Pressed flowers: spirea, fern
Charm: brass bow

General Supplies & Tools

Embroidery hoop
Glue: craft, stick
Iron/ironing board
Needles: embroidery
Paper: tracing
Pencil
Ruler
Scissors: craft; fabric
Toothpicks
Tweezers

Instructions

1. Refer to General
Instructions for Transferring
on page 15. Enlarge Heart
Note Card Transfer Pattern
on opposite page. Center
and transfer design
onto fabric.

2. Place fabric tightly in
embroidery hoop.

3. Refer to General
Instructions for Embroidery
Stitches on pages 10-12.
Using embroidery needle,
embroider flower design
following Heart Note Card
Stitch Guides on
opposite page.

4. Remove from embroidery
hoop. Using fabric scissors,
cut out embroidered hearts.
Using toothpicks and craft
glue, dab a small amount of
glue on gold braided trim.
Attach trim to outer edge of
hearts. Let glue dry.

5. Using fabric scissors, cut
from olive green embroidery
ribbon, one 1½" length, one
3" length, two 5" lengths,
and two 6½" lengths. Press
with iron.

6. Sew 3" ribbon through top center of one heart. Secure opposite end to back of heart with small amount of glue. Let glue dry. Repeat process for 1½" ribbon and second heart.

7. Using pencil and ruler, mark center of note card at top edge above gold trim. Place embroidered hearts on note card. Cross ribbon ends at center mark and glue in place. Glue hearts in place. Let glue dry.

8. Using glue stick, attach 5" and 6½" ribbons to note card, centered between edge of note card and gold trim. Let glue dry. Using craft glue, attach brass bow charm to top center of note card.

9. Using tweezers, place five pressed flowers and two fern pieces in each corner of note card. Using toothpick and a small amount of glue, dab glue on center back of each flower and gently press in

Heart Note Card Placement

Heart Note Card Transfer Pattern   Enlarge 155%

Heart Note Card Stitch Guide

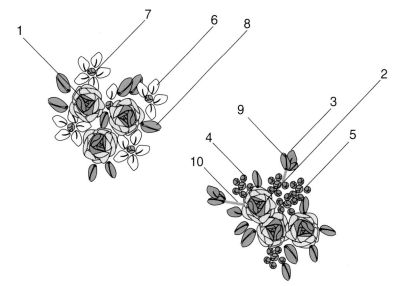

Description		Ribbon	Stitch
1.	Rose Centers	mauve	Spider Web Rose
2.	Rose Petals	soft pink	Spider Web Rose
3.	Rose Buds	soft pink	Straight Stitch
4.	Forget-Me-Not	blue	1-Wrap French Knot
5.	Forget-Me-Not	yellow	1-Wrap French Knot
6.	Daisy Petals	ivory	Straight Stitch
7.	Daisy Centers	yellow	1-Wrap French Knot
8.	Leaves	olive green	Lazy Daisy Stitch
9.	Bud Leaves	olive green	Straight Stitch
10.	Bud Stems	olive green	Twist ribbon tightly

Flower Handkerchief

Materials

Handkerchief: 11" x 11"
  white cotton with
  Battenburg lace
Embroidery ribbon: 2mm
  blue, dk. pink (7 yds.
  each);
  4mm pastel green (5 yds.)
Embroidery floss: green,
  yellow

General Supplies & Tools

Cloth: soft, white
Embroidery hoop
Iron/ironing board
Needles: embroidery;
  hand-sewing
Scissors: fabric
Thread: coordinating

Instructions

1. Using an embroidery
needle and dk. pink
embroidery ribbon, weave
ribbon through lace trim of
handkerchief. Secure ribbon
by folding and weaving 1" of
ribbon end under top ribbon.

2. Using blue embroidery
ribbon, repeat process on
lace corner piece.

3. Refer to General
Instructions for Transferring
on page 15. Use Flower
Handkerchief Transfer
Pattern on opposite page.
Center and transfer design
above lace corner piece of
handkerchief.

4. Place handkerchief
tightly in embroidery hoop.

5. Embroider flower design
following Flower Handkerchief
Stitch Guides on opposite
page.

6. Using hand-sewing
needle and coordinating
thread, tack all loose ribbon
ends on back of handkerchief
with a straight stitch.

7. Remove handkerchief
from embroidery hoop. Place
front side down on soft, white
cloth and press with iron.

Flower Handkerchief Transfer Pattern
Enlarge 110%

Flower Handkerchief Placement

Flower Handkerchief Stitch Guide

Description	Ribbon	Stitch
1. Leaves	pastel green	Satin Stitch
2. Forget-Me-Not	blue	Straight Stitch
3. Forget-Me-Not	yellow floss (1 strand)	1-Wrap French Knot
4. Stems	green floss (1 strand)	Stem Stitch
5. Buds	dk. pink	1-Wrap French Knot

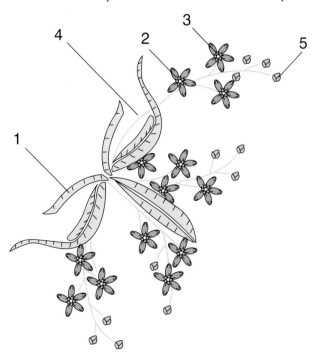

3. Measure up and mark 2½", 3", and 4" from one 14" bottom side and pull six threads at each mark.

4. Using fabric scissors, cut light green embroidery ribbon into three 14"-lengths and two 19"-lengths. Fold each ribbon in half to mark center.

5. Using an embroidery needle, begin weaving from center of one 19" ribbon at center of side row of pulled threads using the following pattern: over five, under three, over five, under three, etc. Repeat process for second side row.

6. Using one 14" ribbon, begin weaving from center of ribbon at center of one bottom row of pulled threads using the following pattern: over eight at center, under three, over five, under three, over five, etc.

7. Using hand-sewing needle and coordinating thread, tack ribbon ends to back of fabric.

Materials
Fabric: 15" x 21" beige
    Monaco (28 count)
Embroidery ribbon: 4mm
    burgundy, lt. green,
    mauve, lt. yellow
    (5 yds. each)
Ribbon rose: cream, small (4)
Embroidery floss: cream

General Supplies & Tools
Needles: embroidery;
    hand-sewing

Pencil: marking
Ruler
Scissors: fabric
Thread: coordinating

Instructions
1. Pull threads to square up Cross-Stitch fabric to 14" x 20".

2. Using ruler and marking pencil, measure in and mark 4" from each 20" side of fabric and pull six threads.

8. Make hem around sides and top of fabric.

9. Fold bottom edge of fabric up ½" and finger press. Fold up again 1" and hem.

10. Center and transfer Tea Cloth Transfer Pattern onto fabric. Refer to General Instructions for Transferring on page 15.

11. Using an embroidery needle, embroider flower pattern following Tea Cloth Stitch Guide. Refer to General Instructions for Embroidery Stitches on pages 10-12.

12. Using hand-sewing needle and coordinating thread, sew premade ribbon roses to fabric. Tack leaves to fabric.with a straight stitch. Refer to Tea Cloth Placement.

Tea Cloth Placement

Tea Cloth Stitch Guide

Step/Description	Ribbon	Stitch
1. Large Daisy	mauve	Japanese Ribbon Stitch
2. Small Daisy	burgundy	Satin Stitch
3. Daisy Centers	yellow	1-wrap French Knot
4. Baby's Breath	cream floss (2 strands)	3-wrap French Knot

Tea Cloth Transfer Pattern
Enlarge   175%

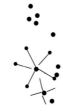

Tea Cloth Stitch Guide

Nature's Bookmark

one 8" and one 2" length. Using glue stick, attach ribbon to left side and bottom of posterboard.

3. Hold maidenhair fern in tweezers. Using toothpick, put a small amount of craft glue on fern and press fern onto posterboard. Refer to Nature's Bookmark Placement as a guide. Repeat process for pink larkspur.

4. Using hole punch, punch a hole in top center of bookmark.

5. Cut 4mm ribbons into 24" pieces. Thread ribbons through bookmark's hole. Tie ribbons together in bow. Knot ribbon ends.

Materials

Pressed flowers and foliage:
  pink larkspur (3),
  maidenhair fern
Embroidery ribbon: 4mm
  rose, olive green,
  burgundy, white (½ yd);
  7mm rose (¾ yd.)
Posterboard: 2" x 8" heavy
  white
Contact paper: 2½" x 9"
  clear (optional)

General Supplies & Tools

Glue: craft; stick
Hole punch
Scissors: craft
Toothpick
Tweezers

Instructions

1. Lay posterboard, shiny side up, on work surface.

2. Using craft scissors, cut rose embroidery ribbon into

Nature's Bookmark Placement

Kelly Henderson

Kelly Henderson has been happily creating since she was four-years-old when she picked up her mother's crochet hook and asked how to use it.

Growing up as the youngest child in a creative family, she was able to glean skills and supplies for needlework, sewing, drawing, painting, and gardening. Her love of these pastimes led to a degree in interior design from Weber State University in Ogden, Utah, and a career as an interior designer.

Kelly loves to build upon the potential she sees in things that are seemingly plain in appearance and gives them new life. With her sense of color, design, and humor, she is able to turn "sows' ears into silk purses."

Kelly designs from her home in Farmington, Utah, where she lives with her daughter, son, and husband, Micheal.

3" x 4½" by wetting edges of note card with water. Place ruler along edge of note card and tear wet edges against ruler.

2. Color rose rubber stamp with dk. mauve and olive green markers and randomly stamp tan note card.

3. Using rubber cement, center and glue tan note card to mauve note card.

4. Leaving a ¼"-wide border, apply soft green adhesive ribbon around mauve note card.

5. Gently twist soft pink wire-edge ribbon. Using a hot glue gun and glue stick, attach ribbon to top of soft green ribbon.

6. Using fabric scissors, cut soft green satin ribbon into two equal lengths. Refer to General Instructions for Folded Leaf on page 8. Using hand-sewing needle and coordinating thread, fold and stitch each ribbon into a folded leaf.

Materials

Note cards: 4½" x 6¼" mauve, 4" x 5¼" tan
Adhesive ribbon: ⅜"-wide soft green (⅔ yd.)
Satin ribbon, ⅜"-wide soft green (⅓ yd.)
Wire-edge ribbon: ⅜"-wide soft pink (⅝ yd.)
Ribbon rose, premade, large: mauve grosgrain (1)
Rubber stamp: rose

General Supplies & Tools

Glue: rubber cement
Hot glue gun and glue sticks
Markers: olive green, dk. mauve
Needles: hand-sewing
Ruler
Scissors: fabric
Thread: coordinating

Instructions

1. Reduce tan note card to

7. Glue leaves to top left corner of note card. Glue mauve grosgrain ribbon rose on top of leaves.

Stamped Note Card Placement

Seeded Eggs

Materials
Styrofoam eggs: 4" (3)
Adhesive ribbon: ⅛"-wide
   mauve, purple (1½ yds.)
Ribbon roses, premade, small
   swirl: fuschia (3), mauve (3),
   purple (3)
Spray sealer: satin-finish
Seed: bird, mustard, sesame

General Supplies & Tools
Glue: craft
Hot glue gun and glue sticks
Paper plates (3)
Scissors: fabric
Toothpicks

Instructions
1. Pour each type of seed onto a separate paper plate.

2. Using craft glue and toothpick, generously spread

glue over the entire surface of one egg.

3. Roll egg on one plate containing one type of

seed until egg is completely covered.

4. Repeat process for remaining eggs and seed types. Let dry.

5. Spray eggs with satin-finish sealer.

6. Using fabric scissors, cut mauve and purple adhesive ribbons into three 18"-lengths. Apply one mauve and one purple ribbon to each egg by wrapping each ribbon lengthwise, around egg twice. Refer to photo and Seeded Eggs Placement.

7. Using hot glue gun and glue stick, attach one fuschia, mauve, and purple swirl ribbon rose to one side of each egg.

Seeded Eggs Placement

Picket Pot

Materials
Terra cotta pot: 5½" diameter
Adhesive ribbon: ⅜"-wide white grosgrain (⅜ yd.); ⅝"-wide white satin (1½ yds.)
Acrylic paint: lt. blue, green, lt. pink, white
Decorating paste: 8 ounces
Spray sealer: satin-finish

General Supplies & Tools
Bags: cake decorating (2)
Cake decorating tips: #3, #66, #101
Couplers: for cake decorating bags (2)
Flower nail
Glue: craft
Knife
Mixing bowls
Paintbrush: 1" flat
Scissors: fabric
Sponge: small

Instructions
1. Using flat paintbrush and light blue acrylic paint, paint terra cotta pot. Let paint dry.

2. Using sponge and white acrylic paint, randomly sponge cloud shapes around top portion of pot.

3. Using fabric scissors, cut

white satin adhesive ribbon into thirteen 4" lengths. Cut one end of each ribbon into a point to resemble a picket. Evenly attach each ribbon picket around pot, leaving ¼" to fold under and attach to bottom of pot as shown in Picket Pot Placement diagram.

4. Apply white grosgrain adhesive ribbon around pot crossing over satin pickets and overlapping ends.

5. In mixing bowl and using knife, mix half of decorating paste with pink acrylic paint following manufacturer's instructions. Repeat process with green acrylic paint.

6. Fill cake decorating bag with pink paste. Cover remaining paste until ready to use.

7. Using cake decorating tip #101 and flower nail, make 12 pink roses. Let dry for several hours.

8. Using craft glue, attach roses between picket fence posts. Make 22 pink buds directly on pot as shown in Picket Pot Placement.

9. Fill second cake decorating bag with green paste. Using tip #66, make leaves directly on pot as shown.

10. Use tip #3 to make tendrils, pasting directly on pot. Refer to Picket Pot Placement. Allow paste to dry.

Picket Pot Placement

Rose Fence

Materials
Picket fence: 13" x 7½" white-washed, premade
Adhesive ribbon: 1½"-wide green check (½ yd.)
Sheer ribbon: ⅝"-wide ivory (1 yd.), pink (1 yd.)
Taffeta ribbon: 1½"-wide green check (1 yd.)
Wire-edge ribbon: ⅞"-wide olive green ombré (5 yds.); 1½"-wide pale yellow (14 yds.)

General Supplies & Tools
Hot glue gun and glue sticks
Needles: hand-sewing
Scissors: fabric
Thread: coordinating

Instructions
1. Using fabric scissors, cut pale yellow wire-edge ribbon into two 16" lengths, three 18" lengths and ten 22" lengths. Refer to General Instructions for Rose on page 8. Make each ribbon into a rose.

2. Cut olive green ombré

wire-edge ribbon into five 4" lengths, five 5½" lengths, and twelve 6½" lengths. Refer to General Instructions for Pulled Leaf on page 9. Using a hand-sewing needle and coordinating thread, fold and stitch each ribbon into pulled leaf.

3. Cut remaining olive green ombré wire-edge ribbon into six 8" lengths. Refer to General Instructions for Tendril on page 9. Tightly twist one ribbon to form a tendril. Repeat process for remaining ribbons. Vary tightness for differing tendril lengths.

4. Using hot glue gun and glue stick, attach roses, leaves, and tendrils to picket fence. Refer to Rose Fence Placement.

5. Cut green check adhesive ribbon into one 16" length. Apply ribbon to bottom of picket fence.

6. Hold remaining ivory and pink sheer, green check taffeta, and pale yellow wire-edge ribbons together as one. Knot both ends. Hot-glue knotted ends to side of picket fence as shown in photo.

Rose Fence Placement

7. Cut ribbons in half at center, overlap about 3" and tie in a knot. Tie pale yellow ribbon in a bow at knot. Trim ribbon ends to 3" tails.

Birthday Cake Box

Needles: hand-sewing
Paintbrush: 1" flat
Scissors: fabric
Thread: coordinating
Pencil

Instructions

1. Using flat paintbrush and white acrylic paint, paint paper maché boxes inside and out. Let dry.

2. Attach ⅞"-wide white grosgrain adhesive ribbon to sides of boxes.

3. Attach ⅜"-wide white grosgrain adhesive ribbon to sides of box lids.

4. Using craft glue, attach small box to top center of large box lid.

5. Lay pink striped sheer ribbon on top of white striped sheer ribbon. Using hand-sewing needle and coordinating thread, run a gather stitch through the bottom edges of ribbons. Pull gather to form ruffle.

Measure, cut, knot, and using hot glue gun and glue stick, attach ruffle to evenly

Materials
Paper maché boxes: 1½" x 3¾" round; 1¾" x 2¾" round
Adhesive ribbon: ⅜"-wide white grosgrain (¾ yd.); ⅞"-wide white grosgrain (¾ yd.)
Satin ribbon, ¹⁄₁₆"-wide: lt. blue (1¾ yds.), lt. pink (1¼ yds.), white (1½ yds.)
Sheer ribbon: ⅜"-wide pink striped (3 yds.); ⅞"-wide white striped (3 yds.);
1⅜"-wide pink (1 yd.)
Ribbon roses, premade: small French blue (25), lt. blue (11), lt. pink (10); small swirl French blue (5), lt. pink (3), white (3)
Cording: ¹⁄₁₆"-wide pink satin (¾ yd.)
Acrylic paint: white

General Supplies & Tools
Glue: craft
Hot glue gun and glue sticks

fit around bottom of large box, bottom of small box, and outside edge of small box lid as shown in Diagram A.

6. Using fabric scissors, cut pink satin cording into one 13½" length and one 10½" length. Glue large length around bottom box at ruffle seam and small length around bottom of small box at ruffle seam.

7. Drape and glue lt. blue, lt. pink and white satin ribbons around top side of small box lid at ten 1" intervals. Drape and glue ribbons around top side of large box lid at ten 1½" intervals. Refer to Birthday Cake Box Placement.

8. Glue a lt. blue ribbon rose, then a French blue ribbon rose, to each draped ribbon interval on top side of small box lid.

9. Glue two French blue ribbon roses and one lt. pink ribbon rose into a cluster and attach to each draped ribbon interval on top side of large box lid.

10. Evenly space and glue French blue swirl ribbon roses to top of ruffle at base of small box as shown in Diagram B.

11. Glue lt. pink and white swirl ribbon roses to ruffle on top of small box lid. Glue six lt. blue ribbon roses in between swirl roses on top of small box lid. Refer to Diagram C.

12. Make pink sheer ribbon into two 3" continuous loops. Glue each loop to top of small box lid as shown in Diagram C. Use a pencil to hold each loop in place as glue cools and dries.

Birthday Cake Box Placement

Diagram A

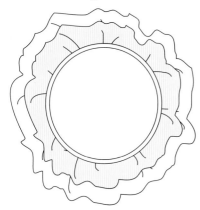

Diagram B

Diagram C

Pedestal Dish

2. Using 1" flat paintbrush and white acrylic paint, paint pedestal and dish.

3. Using a pencil, mark 1" intervals under lip of dish.

4. Dilute lt. green acrylic paint with a small amount of water. Using 1" flat paint-brush, brush a 1" square at every other 1" interval under lip of dish. Paint a second row of green squares under each white square for a checkered pattern.

5. Using ¼" flat paintbrush, paint stripes every ¼" around base of pedestal.

6. Using round paintbrush and metallic gold acrylic paint, paint three gold bands around pedestal as shown in Pedestal Dish Placement on following page.

7. Using fabric scissors, cut nine 2" lengths and one 26" length of soft green satin adhesive ribbon. Refer to Pedestal Dish Placement. Diagonally attach each small ribbon every ½" around rounded portion of pedestal.

Materials
Pedestal: 4" x 4½" terra cotta
Plant dish: 8½" diameter terra cotta, rounded
Adhesive ribbon: ¼"-wide soft green satin (1⅓ yds.)
Ribbon roses, premade, small: dk. mauve (13), lt. pink (6)
Acrylic paint: lt. green, metallic gold, white
Spray sealer: polyurethane satin-finish

General Supplies & Tools
Scissors: fabric
Glue: craft
Hot glue gun and glue sticks
Paintbrush: ¼" and 1" flat; ¼" round
Pencil
Sandpaper: medium grid

Instructions
1. Using sandpaper, lightly sand terra cotta pedestal and plant dish.

8. Attach remaining ribbon around top lip of dish.

9. Using a hot glue gun and glue sticks, attach seven dk. mauve ribbon roses around pedestal. Refer to Pedestal Dish Placement.

10. Glue remaining dk. mauve and lt. pink ribbon roses to top row of green squares, alternating colors.

11. Using craft glue, secure dish to pedestal. Let dry.

12. Spray completed project with two coats of polyurethane satin-finish sealer.

Pedestal Dish Placement

Optional Color Combination

Pumpkin

Materials

Wire pumpkin: 9"
Adhesive ribbon, ⅞"-wide: woven copper metallic wire-edge (10 yds.)
Wire-edge ribbon: ⅞"-wide olive green ombré (2 yds.); 1½"-wide brown ombré (2 yds.); woven copper metallic (3 yds.)

General Supplies & Tools

Hot glue gun and glue sticks
Needles: hand-sewing

Pencil
Scissors: fabric; craft
Thread: coordinating

Instructions

1. Beginning at base, wrap woven copper metallic wire-edge adhesive ribbon around each spoke of wire pumpkin.

2. Wrap woven copper metallic wire-edge ribbon around top and bottom bases of pumpkin. Wrap in a clockwise manner and wrap twice between spokes. Secure ribbon at beginning and end with hot glue.

3. Using fabric scissors, cut brown ombré wire-edge ribbon into five 9½" lengths, and three 8" lengths. Cut olive green ombré wire-edge ribbon into two 9" lengths, one 7" length and one 6" length. Refer to General Instructions for Pulled Leaf on page 9. Using a hand-sewing needle and a length of coordinating thread, fold and stitch each ribbon into a pulled leaf.

4. Cut olive green ombré wire-edge ribbon into two 8" lengths, one 10" length and one 12" length. Refer to General Instructions for Tendril on page 9. Tightly twist each ribbon to form a tendril.

5. With remaining olive green ombré ribbon, wrap pumpkin stem.

6. Glue brown leaves to top base of pumpkin. Glue green leaves and tendrils to top of brown leaves.

Top View

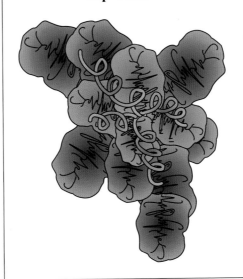

Pumpkin Placement

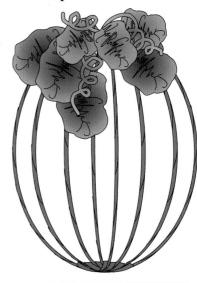

Baby Dress

Materials
Baby underwear: one-piece, newborn
Fabric: pink seersucker (⅓ yd.)
Adhesive ribbon: ⅜"-wide pink check (2 yds.); 1½"-wide pink floral (½ yd.)

General Supplies & Tools
Iron/ironing board
Measuring tape
Needles: hand-sewing
Pencil
Scissors: fabric
Sewing machine
Straight pins
Thread: coordinating

Instructions

1. Using fabric scissors, cut pink check adhesive ribbon into two 8" lengths, two 16" lengths and one 19" length.

2. Measure down 7" from front right shoulder and in 1¼" from front side of underwear and mark. Repeat process for left shoulder.

3. Measure down 7" from back right shoulder and in 2" from back side of underwear and mark.

measures 6". Cut length to 35". Press folded edge. Refer to Diagram B.

7. Fold fabric in half lengthwise. Sew a ⅜" seam along 6" sides. Sew two rows of gathering stitches ¼" from top edge of fabric. Refer to Diagram C.

8. Refer to Diagram D. Tightly gather fabric to fit around waist of underwear. Center seam at back of underwear.

9. Using straight pins, pin gathered fabric at 7" mark around waist.

10. Apply pink floral adhesive ribbon around waist, beginning at center back. Attach half of it to gathered fabric and half to underwear. Remove pins as ribbon is applied.

11. Press all adhesive ribbons according to manufacturer's instructions.

4. Apply 16" ribbons to front side of underwear, beginning at front marks, running straight up to shoulders, criss-crossing over back, and ending at back marks; see Diagram A.

5. Apply 8" ribbons around edges of sleeves, beginning and ending at inside seam of sleeve as in Diagram A.

6. Fold pink seersucker fabric in half so width

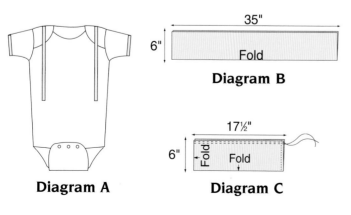

Diagram A

35"

6"

Fold

Diagram B

17½"

6"

Fold   Fold

Diagram C

Diagram D (front)

Diagram D (back)

12. Cut 19" ribbon into two equal lengths. Press ribbons together to form one double-faced ribbon. Tie ribbon into bow. Refer to General Instructions for Fork Cut on page 8. Fork-cut ribbon ends. Using hand-sewing needle and coordinating thread, tack bow to center front of neck.

Baby Dress Placement

Toddler Coat

Materials

Sweatshirt: red crewneck, child's small

Adhesive ribbon: ⅞"-wide green/red plaid (3 yds.); 1½"-wide green/red polka dot print (½ yd.), Scottie dog print (¼ yd.)

Grosgrain ribbon: 1"-wide green/red stripe with gold edging (1½ yds.)

General Supplies & Tools

Iron/ironing board
Ruler
Scissors: fabric
Straight pins

Instructions

1. Fold sweatshirt in half. Using straight pins, pin side seams, shoulder seams and center front as shown in Diagram A on following page. Using fabric scissors, cut down center front to create a cardigan.

2. Cut off cuffs and waistband.

3. Beginning at top right edge of neck, apply green/red plaid adhesive ribbon by folding ribbon over raw edge of center front, bottom, and opposite side of center front. Miter ribbon at lower front

corners as shown in Diagram B. Repeat process for sleeves, beginning and ending at seams.

4. Fold one end of green/red stripe with gold edging grosgrain ribbon under 1½". Refer to General Instructions for Knife Pleating on page 9. Using ruler, begin pleating ribbon around neck edge. Pin to hold in place.

5. Apply green/red plaid adhesive ribbon over top ¼" of pleated ribbon, leaving ½" to turn under at beginning and end of neck edge. Remove pins as ribbon is applied.

6. Apply green/red plaid adhesive ribbon to inside of neck edge, matching edges and ends of top ribbon. Fold ribbon ends to inside of neck edge.

7. Using Scottie Dog Pattern, cut out six Scottie dogs from Scottie dog print adhesive ribbon. At ½" intervals from front edge of cardigan, apply three dogs to each front side, 3" from bottom edge. Refer to Toddler Coat Placement.

8. Using Polka Dot Pattern, cut out 20 polka dots from green/red plaid polka dot print adhesive ribbon. At ½" intervals, apply five polka dots above and below each set of Scottie dogs.

9. Press all adhesive ribbons according to manufacturer's instructions.

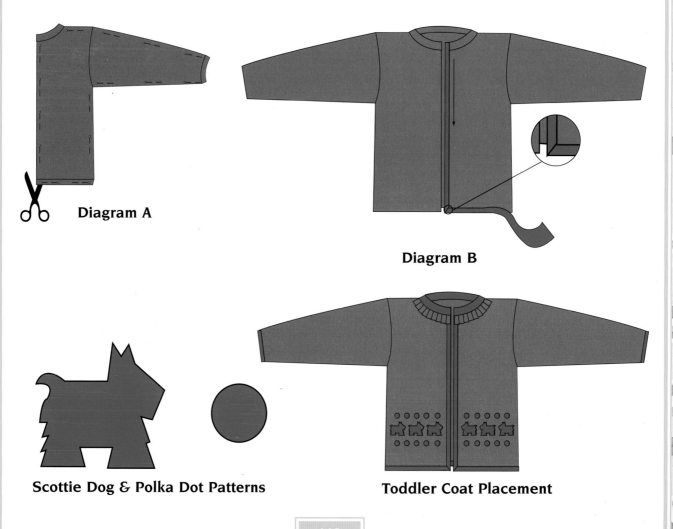

Diagram A

Diagram B

Scottie Dog & Polka Dot Patterns

Toddler Coat Placement

2. Using pencil, trace four picket fence post patterns onto ¼" pine. Using scroll saw, cut out wooden picket fence post pieces.

3. Using a pencil and a wooden picket fence post piece as a pattern, trace on wrong side of fabric eight times, enlarging fabric fence posts by ⅛". Using fabric scissors, cut out fence posts.

4. Using spray adhesive, spray front of each fence post. Attach fabric to each fence post, smoothing any wrinkles or bubbles. Repeat process for backs of posts.

5. Using craft glue, attach fabric edges to sides of posts.

6. Cut soft green adhesive ribbon into four 54" lengths and eighteen 8½" lengths. Loosely apply short ribbons in a criss-cross manner on front of each fence post, tucking ribbon ends onto sides of fence posts. Refer to Diagram A on following

Materials

Picket fence posts, pine:
   6" x 22" x ¼" (4)
Fabric: 54"-wide home
   decorating (1 yd.)
Adhesive ribbon: ¼"-wide
   soft green (10¼ yds.)
Ribbon roses, premade,
   large: ivory blooming (12);
   ivory ruffle (6)
Hinges: ¼" x ¾" (6)

General Supplies & Tools

Drill, assorted drill bits
Glue: craft; spray adhesive
Hot glue gun and glue sticks
Pencil
Saw: scroll
Scissors: fabric
Screwdriver

Instructions

1. Enlarge Pattern A on following page on copy machine by 480%.

page. Apply each long ribbon around all sides of fence posts.

**Pattern A/Diagram A
Enlarge 480%**

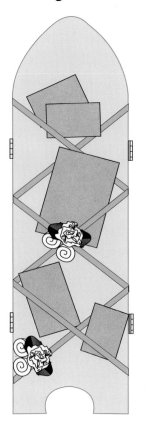

7. Lay fence posts side-by-side. From bottom of fence posts, measure and mark hinge placement on sides of fence posts at 4¼" and 14¾".

8. Using a drill and screwdriver, drill holes for hinges and screw hinges in place. Attach center hinges opposite of others so screen folds accordion-style.

9. Make six rose clusters with two ivory blooming and one ivory ruffle rose in each cluster. Using a hot glue gun and glue stick, attach clusters to fence

posts. Refer to Folding Screen Placement.

10. Slip photographs into loosely applied crossed ribbons as desired. Press ribbon with fingers to secure.

Folding Screen Placement

Candle Spray

Materials
Candle: 3" x 6" white
Adhesive ribbon: 1½"-wide black grosgrain (⅜ yd.)
Sheer ribbon: ⅞"-wide white with gold trim (⅔ yd.); 1½"-wide black with gold trim (⅔ yd.)
Wire-edge ribbon: 1½"-wide olive green ombré (⅔ yd.)
Ribbon rose, premade, large:

burgundy petal (1)
Corrugated craft paper: 3½" x 10½"

General Supplies & Tools
Hot glue gun and glue sticks
Needle: hand-sewing
Scissors: fabric
Thread: coordinating

Instructions
1. Wrap corrugated craft paper around candle. Using hot glue gun and glue sticks, seal paper ends together.

2. Attach black grosgrain adhesive ribbon around center of corrugated paper.

3. Lay white with gold trim sheer ribbon in center of black with gold trim sheer ribbon. Wrap both ribbons around center of black grosgrain ribbon and tie into bow as shown in Diagram A on opposite page. Secure bow to black grosgrain ribbon with a dab of hot glue.

Diagram A

Diagram B

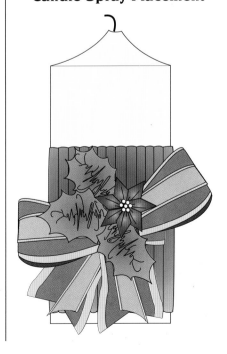

Candle Spray Placement

4. Using fabric scissors, cut olive green ombré wire-edge ribbon into one 8" length, one 7" length and one 6" length. Refer to General Instructions for Pulled Leaf on page 9. Using hand-sewing needle and coordinating thread, fold and stitch each ribbon into a pulled leaf. Pinch edges of leaves to resemble holly leaves as shown in Diagram B.

5. Glue leaves on center top of bow. Glue burgundy petal ribbon rose to leaves as shown in Diagram C.

Diagram C

Scissors: fabric
Sewing machine
Thread: coordinating

Instructions

1. Enlarge Pattern A on opposite page on copy machine by 400%.

2. Using pencil, trace two stocking patterns onto both the tapestry and muslin fabrics. Using fabric scissors, cut out stocking patterns.

3. With ⅜" seam, sew muslin stockings together, leaving top open.

4. With ⅜" seam and right sides together, sew tapestry stockings together, leaving top open. Turn right side out.

5. Insert muslin stocking into tapestry stocking. Turn top edges on stockings inside ¼". Using a hand-sewing needle and coordinating thread, stitch muslin and tapestry together.

6. Cut cording into one 5" length as shown in Diagram

Materials

Fabric: sage green tapestry
(⅓ yd.); muslin (⅓ yd.)
Adhesive ribbon: ⅜"-wide
cream fleur (1½ yds.), soft
green satin (1½ yds.)
Wire-edge ribbon: ⅞"-wide
olive green ombré (¾ yd.),
purple/green ombré
(3 yds.); 1½"-wide
gold/white striped
(1⅓ yds.), lavender (2 yds.),
purple ombré

(1⅓ yds.), iridescent
purple/gold (1⅓ yds.)
Ribbon rose, premade:
small iridescent purple
petal (3); medium
iridescent purple (10)
Cording: ⅛"-wide ivory satin
(1½ yds.)

General Supplies & Tools

Hot glue gun and glue sticks
Needles: hand-sewing
Pencil

A. Loop cording and stitch to top back seam of stocking. Using a hot glue gun and glue stick, attach remaining cording around side seams and around top opening of stocking.

7. Cut lavender wire-edge ribbon into three 22" lengths. Refer to General Instructions for Rose on page 9. Make each ribbon into a rose.

8. Cut purple/green ombré wire-edge ribbon into one 22" length, two 18" lengths, two 16" lengths, one 10" length and one 6" length. Make each ribbon into a rose. Pull wire on green edge of ribbon.

9. Cut olive green ombré wire-edge ribbon into three 7" lengths and one 4½" length. Refer to General Instructions for Pulled Leaf on page 9. Fold and stitch each ribbon into a pulled leaf.

10. Attach cream fleur and soft green satin adhesive ribbon to front of stocking in a woven fashion as shown in Tapestry Stocking Placement.

11. Glue flowers and leaves to front top of stocking.

12. Hold gold/white striped, purple ombré, and iridescent purple/gold wire-edge ribbons together as one. Cut ribbons in half. Tie ribbons into two bows. Tie bows together with small piece of purple ombré ribbon.

13. Hot glue bows to top back edge of stocking.

14. Refer to General Instructions for Fork Cut on page 8. Fork-cut ribbon ends. Shape and twist tails.

**Pattern A/Diagram A
Enlarge 400%**

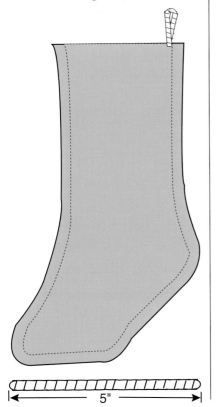

5"

Tapestry Stocking Placement

Paintbrush: 1" flat
Scissors: craft; fabric

Instructions

1. Using white acrylic paint and flat paintbrush, paint step and inside of gazebo. Let dry.

2. Using craft scissors, cut wrapping paper to fit each panel of gazebo roof.

3. Using spray adhesive, spray gazebo roof. Attach wrapping paper panels to roof.

4. Measure and cut one piece of wrapping paper to fit around gazebo walls.

5. Spray walls with spray adhesive and attach paper.

6. Using craft knife, cut out door, windows and lattice holes from inside gazebo, leaving a small amount of paper to turn inside. Clip corners. Using craft glue, glue inside edge of door, windows, and lattice holes. Press excess paper inside.

7. Using fabric scissors, cut

Materials

Gazebo: 8" x 10" paper maché
Adhesive ribbon: ⅜"-wide ivory fleur (1½ yds.), white grosgrain (3 yds.); ⅛"-wide white grosgrain (1½ yds.)
Lace ribbon: ⅞"-wide white (¾ yd.)
Satin ribbon: ¼"-wide white picot-edge (2½ yards); ½"-wide white picot-edge (½ yd.)

Sheer ribbon: ⅝"-wide white stripe picot-edge (¾ yd.)
Ribbon roses, premade: small ivory (3), white (4); large white blooming (1)
Acrylic paint: white
Wrapping paper: ivory and tan print

General Supplies & Tools

Glue: craft; spray adhesive
Hot glue gun and glue sticks
Knife: craft

¼"-wide white picot-edge satin ribbon into strips to make lattice pattern beneath windows and around door. Using craft glue, attach strips to gazebo. Refer to Satin Gazebo Placement.

8. Cut ⅜"-wide white grosgrain adhesive ribbon into eight 6" lengths and eight 5" lengths. Apply 6" ribbons to corners of wall panels. Apply 5" ribbons to corners of roof panels.

9. Cut ⅞"-wide white grosgrain adhesive ribbon into eight 3" lengths and one 25" length. Apply 25" ribbon around eaves, folding excess ribbon underneath eaves. Diagonally cut ribbon ends to fit the underside of each eaves panel.

10. Cut ivory fleur adhesive ribbon into one 25" length. Center and apply ribbon around eaves on top of white grosgrain adhesive ribbon.

11. Using a hot glue gun and glue stick, attach white lace ribbon to bottom edge of roof.

12. Glue ½"-wide white picot-edge satin ribbon around bottom of windows.

13. Apply remaining ⅜"-wide white grosgrain adhesive ribbon around bottom of lattice.

14. Using craft glue, attach sheer white picot-edge ribbon around bottom side of step. Center and apply

remaining ivory fleur adhesive ribbon over sheer ribbon.

15. Using hot glue, attach large white blooming ribbon rose to top of roof. Glue small ivory and white ribbon roses around door as desired.

Satin Gazebo Placement

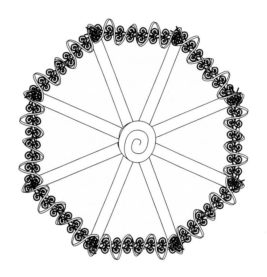

Top View

2. Attach soft green satin adhesive ribbon around sides of box lid.

3. Attach burgundy satin adhesive ribbon around top and bottom edges of soft green ribbon as shown in Trinket Box Placement on opposite page.

4. Using a hand-sewing needle and coordinating thread, run a gather stitch down the center of the taupe with gold edge sheer ribbon. Pull gathers until ribbon fits top of box lid.

5. Using a hot glue gun and glue sticks, attach gathered ribbon to corner points on box lid.

6. Glue clusters of three ribbon roses on top of gathered ribbon at corner points of box lid.

7. Using pencil, center and trace box lid onto picture insert. Using craft scissors, cut out picture and fit into box lid. Using rubber cement, glue inside lid backing to picture.

Materials

Box: 3¼" geometric paper maché with insertable lid
Adhesive ribbon: ⅛"-wide burgundy satin (1⅛ yd.); ⅜"- wide soft green satin (20")
Sheer ribbon: ⅜"-wide taupe with gold edge (1⅔ yds.)
Ribbon roses, premade, small: burgundy (18)
Acrylic paint: metallic gold
Spray sealer: matte-finish
Picture insert

General Supplies & Tools

Glue: rubber cement
Hot glue gun and glue sticks
Needles: hand-sewing
Paintbrush: 1" flat
Pencil
Scissors: craft
Thread: coordinating

Instructions

1. Using metallic gold acrylic paint, paint geometric paper maché box. Let dry.

Trinket Box Placement

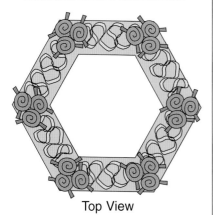

Top View

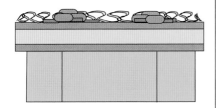

Penny Purse

Materials
Adhesive ribbon: 1½"-wide
 burgundy check (¼ yd.)
Sheer ribbon: ⅝"-wide ivory
 striped picot-edge (¼ yd.)
Velvet ribbon: ³⁄₁₆"-wide
 burgundy (1 yd.)
Wire-edge ribbon: 2⅞"-wide
 iridescent burgundy (½ yd.)
Ribbon rose, premade, large:
 iridescent burgundy petal
Snap

General Supplies & Tools
Needles: hand-sewing
Scissors: fabric; craft
Thread: coordinating

Diagram A
Top Edges

Fold

Raw Edges

Diagram B
Top Edges

Fold

Raw Edges

Fold

Instructions
1. Using craft scissors, cut iridescent burgundy wire-edge ribbon into two 8"-lengths. Gently pull to remove wire.

2. Fold one ribbon in half lengthwise. With a ¼" seam and using a hand-sewing needle and coordinating thread, stitch around three edges as in Diagram A.

3. Fold second ribbon so raw edges overlap at center. With ¼" seam, stitch raw edges and bottom edge of ribbon. Refer to Diagram B.

4. Turn both ribbons right side out. Tack one top edge of first ribbon and top edges of second ribbon together. Fold top flap over to form penny purse.

5. Attach burgundy check adhesive ribbon to bottom edge of purse flap, beginning and ending at inside center back of flap.

6. Center ivory striped picot-edge sheer ribbon on burgundy check ribbon. Tack ribbon ends to burgundy check ribbon at inside center seam of flap.

7. Using hand sewing needle and coordinating thread, attach ribbon petal rose to ribbons at center front of flap.

8. Measure velvet ribbon around neck and cut to desired length. Sew ribbon ends to inside corner edges of purse, just above seam.

9. Sew snap to inside flap and corresponding area of purse pocket.

Penny Purse Placement

Floral Angel

Materials

Doll: 13" muslin with bendable arms and legs

Doll hair: rust (1 package)

Fabric, torn: 9" x 20" ivory and pink mini print; 4" x 8" ivory and tan mini print (all fabric edges should be ragged)

Adhesive ribbon: ⅝"-wide green satin (¾ yd.)

Craft ribbon: 1½"-wide tan and green check (1¼ yd.)

Satin ribbon: ¹⁄₁₆"-wide ivory (⅔ yd.)

Sheer ribbon: ⅞"-wide green with gold edge (½ yd.); 1½"-wide floral (1¼ yds.)

Wire-edge ribbon: ⅜"-wide green (⅓ yd.)

Ribbon roses, premade: small cinnamon (15), rust (10); small ruffle cinnamon (4)

Double fan bow: teal

Birds: 1½" blue (2)

Pot: miniature clay or wood

Garden spade: miniature

Stuffing

General Supplies & Tools

Glue: fabric
Hot glue gun and glue sticks
Needles: hand-sewing
Scissors: fabric
Thread: coordinating
Toothpick

Instructions

All seams are ¼".

1. If constructing muslin doll, using fabric scissors, cut pieces as indicated using Doll Pattern at right.

2. With right sides together, stitch Body Front to Back leaving bottom open for stuffing. Stuff firmly and slip-stitch opening closed. Repeat process for Left Leg, Right Leg, Left Arm, Right Arm, and Head.

3. Tack Left Leg and Right Leg to bottom of Body. Tack Left Arm and Right Arm to respective sides of Body. Tack back of Head to front neck area of Body.

4. Fold ivory and pink mini print fabric in half length-wise, right sides together. Using a hand-sewing needle and coordinating thread, stitch 9" sides of fabric together to form a skirt. Turn right side out.

5. Gather-stitch around one

raw edge of skirt. Put doll inside skirt and tightly gather skirt around doll's waist. Tack skirt to doll's body.

6. Tear ivory and tan mini print fabric in half so each piece is 2" x 8". Fold each fabric piece in half length-wise. Criss-cross fabric pieces across doll's chest to back to form a bodice.

7. Cut tan and green check craft ribbon into eight 5" pieces. Using fabric glue, secure one long edge of each ribbon piece to overlap all but ½" of previous ribbon's

Doll Pattern   Enlarge 200%

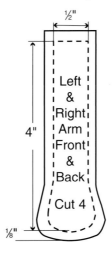

½"

Left
&
Right
Arm
Front
&
Back

Cut 4

4"

⅛"

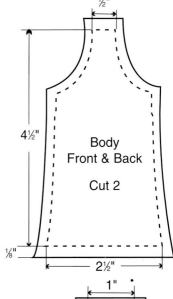

½"

Body
Front & Back

Cut 2

4½"

⅛"

2½"

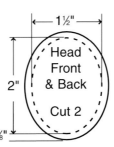

1½"

Head
Front
& Back

Cut 2

2"

⅛"

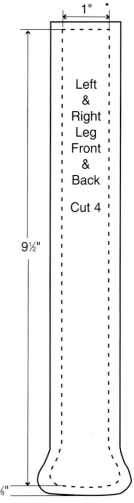

1"

Left
&
Right
Leg
Front
&
Back

Cut 4

9½"

⅛"

long edge, matching plaids until all ribbons are used. Trim top and bottom ends into even curves. Refer to apron on Floral Angel Placement.

8. Secure bodice and apron to doll's waist by attaching 3" of green satin adhesive ribbon around doll's waist.

9. Using a hot glue gun and glue sticks, attach teal fan bow to center of green satin waistband.

10. Tie floral and green with gold edge sheer ribbons into bows. Glue bows to back of doll for wings.

11. Glue cinnamon ruffle ribbon roses to inside of pot. Glue one bird to roses.

12. Glue miniature garden spade to palm of doll's right hand. Glue back of spade to pot. Glue left arm around pot.

13. Wrap and twist green wire-edge ribbon into a 1½" diameter halo. Hold halo against top of toothpick and continue wrapping ribbon around toothpick to form the halo stem.

14. Glue rust ribbon roses

and 13 cinnamon ribbon roses around halo. Glue remaining bird to halo. Glue halo to back of doll's head.

15. Glue doll hair to doll's head.

16. Using fabric scissors, cut remaining green satin

adhesive ribbon into two equal lengths. Attach ribbons to doll's feet.

17. Cut ivory satin ribbon into two equal lengths. Lace each ribbon around doll's ankles and tie into bow. Glue a cinnamon ribbon rose to each bow.

Floral Angel Placement

Ladybug Gift Bag

Materials
Paper maché bag: 5" x 6"
Grosgrain ribbon: ¼"-wide
  dk. green (¼ yd.); 1"-wide
  red with black polka dot
  (1½ yds.), green (½ yd.)
Satin ribbon: ¾"-wide white
  wire-edge (1 yd.)
Acrylic paints: black, dk. red,
  yellow
Buttons: ½" black (1); ⅝"
  yellow (3)

General Supplies & Tools
Hot glue gun and glue sticks
Needles: hand-sewing
Paintbrush: medium
Pen: black felt marker
Scissors: fabric
Thread: white

Instructions
1. Using medium
paintbrush and black acrylic
paint, paint sides, bottom
and ¼" of bottom front of
paper maché bag. Using dk.
red acrylic paint, paint inside
of bag. Using yellow acrylic
paint, paint front and back
of bag.

2. Using black felt marker,
write lettering on front of
bag. Refer to Ladybug Gift
Bag Placement on following
page.

3. Using fabric scissors, cut
dk. green grosgrain ribbon
into one 1¼" length, one 1½"
length and one 1¾" length
for stems. Using hot glue
gun and glue stick, attach
stems to front of bag.

4. Cut green grosgrain
ribbon into three equal
lengths. Knot each ribbon in
center. Cut each ribbon end
into a rounded point for
leaves. Glue leaves to stems.

5. Cut white wire-edge satin
ribbon into one 12" length,
one 10" length and one 8"
length. Using a hand-sewing
needle and white thread, run
a gather stitch along one
edge of each ribbon. Gather
thread to form a circular
flower. Tack ribbon ends

together. Sew a yellow button in center of each flower. Glue flowers to top of stems.

6. Cut a 2" length of red with black polka dot grosgrain ribbon into two 1" x ½" half circles for body of ladybug. Glue to front of bag. Glue black button to ladybug for head. Draw flight pattern with black magic marker.

7. Cut red with black polka dot grosgrain ribbon into one 5" length. Glue to bottom of bag, at edge of black strip and covering ends of stems.

8. Cut remaining red with black polka dot ribbon into two equal lengths. Knot each ribbon through holes in bag for handles. Refer to General Instructions for Fork Cut on page 8. Fork-cut ribbon ends.

Ladybug Gift Bag Placement

Lady bug fly away...

Materials
Accordion file folder: 7½" x 9½"
Craft ribbon: ⅜"-wide red/tan check (1½ yds.); 1"-wide green/tan check (¼ yd.); 1¼"-wide blue/tan check (⅜ yd.)
Cardboard: 8" x 10" (2)
Fabric: 9½" x 11½" muslin (2)
Twine: ⅛ yd.

General Supplies & Tools
Hot glue gun and glue sticks
Pens: black and brown fine tip markers
Scissors: fabric; scalloped-edge

Instructions
1. Using hot glue gun and glue stick, wrap and secure muslin fabric pieces to one side of each cardboard piece. Label cardboard pieces front and back.

2. Using fabric scissors, cut blue/tan check craft ribbon into one 10" length. Using scalloped-edge scissors, cut along top and bottom edges of ribbon. Glue ribbon ½" above bottom edge of front cardboard.

3. Using fabric scissors and Pattern A on opposite page, cut red/tan check craft ribbon into pieces for

three apples. Cut green/tan check craft ribbon for six leaves. Arrange and glue to front of cardboard. Refer to Apple-a-Day Placement.

4. Cut twine into three equal lengths. Knot each piece of twine for stem and glue in place with knot down on apple.

5. Using black fine tip marker, draw stitching lines around apples and border.

6. Using brown fine tip marker, write lettering on front.

7. Center and glue cardboard pieces to front and back of accordion file folder.

8. Cut remaining red/tan check craft ribbon into two equal lengths. Center and glue one end of each ribbon to inside top front and back edge of folder. Tie ribbons into a bow to close folder.

Pattern A   Enlarge 190%

Apple-a-Day Placement

Metric Equivalency Chart
mm-millimetres cm-centimetres
inches to millimetres and centimetres

inches	mm	cm	inches	cm	inches	cm
⅛	3	0.3	9	22.9	30	76.2
¼	6	0.6	10	25.4	31	78.7
½	13	1.3	12	30.5	33	83.8
⅝	16	1.6	13	33.0	34	86.4
¾	19	1.9	14	35.6	35	88.9
⅞	22	2.2	15	38.1	36	91.4
1	25	2.5	16	40.6	37	94.0
1¼	32	3.2	17	43.2	38	96.5
1½	38	3.8	18	45.7	39	99.1
1¾	44	4.4	19	48.3	40	101.6
2	51	5.1	20	50.8	41	104.1
2½	64	6.4	21	53.3	42	106.7
3	76	7.6	22	55.9	43	109.2
3½	89	8.9	23	58.4	44	111.8
4	102	10.2	24	61.0	45	114.3
4½	114	11.4	25	63.5	46	116.8
5	127	12.7	26	66.0	47	119.4
6	152	15.2	27	68.6	48	121.9
7	178	17.8	28	71.1	49	124.5
8	203	20.3	29	73.7	50	127.0

Index

Angel Gift...20
Angel Pillow..31
Apple-a-Day...126
Baby Dress...109
Bee Stationery...50
Bird Bath Picture.....................................73
Birthday Cake Box..................................105
Candlelight..53
Candle Spray..114
Cat Cut-Out..17
Checked Hearts Towel.............................70
Desk Set...62
Dogwood Pillow......................................89
Fern Journal..68
Floral Angel...122
Flower Basket..84
Flower Handkerchief................................94
Folding Screen.......................................113
Friendship Garden Girl.............................27
General Instructions.............................8-15
  Dimensional Ribbon Work....................8-10
    Folded Leaf..8
    Folded Rose...8
    Fork Cut..8
    Free Form Flower..................................8
    Gather Stitch..8
    Knife Pleating.......................................9
    Pulled Leaf...9
    Rose...9
    Tendril..9
  Embroidery Basics...............................9-10
    End Stitching...9
    Floss...9
    Knotting End of Ribbon..........................9
    Needles...9
    Ribbon Tips...10
    Threading Ribbon.................................10
  Embroidery Stitches............................10-12
    Backstitch...10
    Blanket Stitch......................................10
    Cross-Stitch..10

Decorative Lazy Daisy Stitch...................10
French Knot..10
Japanese Ribbon Stitch...........................10
Lazy Daisy Stitch.....................................10
Leaf Stitch..11
Long Stitch...11
Outline Stitch..11
Padded Satin Stitch.................................11
Padded Straight Stitch.............................11
Running Stitch..11
Satin Stitch...11
Spider Web Rose.....................................11
Stem Stitch...12
Straight Stitch...12
Fabric Basics...12
  Fusible Appliqué....................................12
  Pressing Fabric......................................12
  Tea-dying..12
Pressed Flowers...................................12-13
  Pressing Flowers.................................12-13
  Creativity..13
  Glossary of Flowers................................13
Ribbon Amounts......................................13
Stamping on Ribbon Basics...................13-14
  Embossing...13-14
  Inks..14
  Ribbons...14
  Stamps..14
Tool Basics..14-15
  Fabric Scissors.......................................14
  Floss...14
  Heat Tool...14-15
  Hot Glue Gun & Glue Sticks....................15
  Marking Tools...15
  Soft Rubber Brayer..................................15
Transferring...15
  Materials...15
  Tools...15
Wood Basics..15
  Painting Techniques................................15
  Transferring to Wood...............................15

Gift Wrap..54
Green Pillow..49
Heart Note Card......................................92
Henderson, Kelly......................................99
Initial...77
Kitchen Magnets......................................48
Ladybug Gift Bag....................................125
Lemon & Chili Bags.................................45
Merry Heart...33
Metric Equivalency................................128
Nature's Bookmark...................................98
Oriental Pillows.......................................64
Peace Angel..35
Pedestal Dish...107
Penny Purse...121
Photo Albums..57
Picket Pot..102
Picture Hanger..65
Potted Salvia...82
Pumpkin..108
Rain or Shine...23
Ribbon Quilt..61
Ribbon Topiary..60
Rose Fence..103
Saffiote, Cheri...16
Satin Gazebo...118
Seeded Eggs..101
Snowfolk..38
Snow Cut-Out...40
Snuggs, Ann...72
Stamped Note Card................................100
Sunflower Journal....................................71
Sweet Home Journal................................55
Taormina, Grace......................................44
Tapestry Stocking...................................116
Tea Cloth..96
Toddler Coat..111
Trinket Box..120
Velvet Pillow...56
Very Cherry...66
Welcome...86
Zebra Frame..52